Pra..

M000045897

MOTHERS CAN'T BE EVERYWHERE BUT GOD IS

"Alice Scott-Ferguson has written the quintessential book on motherhood. I don't know which is the greater treasure, the wisdom she imparts or the lyrical language she uses. Every woman who takes her role as a mother seriously needs to read this book."

–NANCY PARKER BRUMMETT
Author
IT TAKES A HOME, TAKE MY HAND AGAIN, and A WOMAN'S DAILY PRAYER BOOK

"If you're feeling overwhelmed or insecure in your mothering, then this book is for you. Alice Scott-Ferguson's ... speak-the-truth-in-love approach will cause you to think, "God is in control and He's helping me even more than I realize. I can do this!"

–KATHY COLLARD MILLER
Speaker, Author
WHY DO I PUT SO MUCH PRESSURE ON MYSELF?

"*Mothers Can't Be Everywhere, But God Is,* has spoken to this grandmother's heart. It applied a balm to many of the lingering regrets from my child-rearing years. I wish I had had the book then. Alice Scott-Ferguson's perspective transcends the traditional and leads her reader into liberty. Thanks, Alice. It is simply profound."

–TIPI CHARLES
Reader in Colorado

"Alice Scott-Ferguson is a thinking woman who has named the things that get mothers into trouble—hovering, meddling, expecting our children to prove our worth—all in the effort to be a perfect parent. Thank you, Alice, for helping us trust God and let our parenting be about our children instead of being about us."

–JAN JOHNSON
Speaker, Author
GROWING COMPASSIONATE KIDS
and *WHEN THE SOUL LISTENS*

"Alice Scott-Ferguson has written a book that frees women from the burden of trying to be the "perfect mother." With her unique blend of spiritual maturity and practical Scottish wisdom, Alice uncovers the simple truth about parenting and it is this: God's children are only taken care of by Christ who lives in us. Whether you are a first-time mom or a veteran grandmother, a step-mom or an unwed pregnant teen, this book will bless you. Read it!"

–MARY CLAIRE BLAKEMAN
Co-Author
SAFE HOMES, SAFE NEIGHBORHOODS

"It's a great book, easy to read in small segments, which is what mothers need. ... It gave me hope. For too long single mothers like me have been carrying too heavy a load."

–SUE BRESNAHAN
Reader in Ohio

"This book was encouraging to me, it helped me to realize I cannot be there all the time for my children. As they are growing and making their own decisions, God is there and he will guide you and them. It was an easy read. I enjoyed it."

–ONLINE REVIEWER

MOTHERS
CAN'T BE EVERYWHERE
BUT GOD IS

A Liberating Look
at Motherhood

Alice Scott-Ferguson

CLADACH
PUBLISHING

MOTHERS CAN'T BE EVERYWHERE
BUT GOD IS:
A LIBERATING LOOK AT MOTHERHOOD

Published by
CLADACH Publishing
PO Box 336144 Greeley, CO 80633
http://cladach.com

Cover Art Copyright © Amy Whitehouse
Learn more about "Amy Whitehouse Fine Art" at:
http://AmyWhitehousePaintings.com

Author Photo by Grant Ferguson

ISBN 978-0-9670386-7-4

Library of Congress Control Number: 2002114420

Printed in the United States of America

To the memory of
my mother,
Mary Jane Scott,
who, in her lifetime, exemplified
God's grace, love, and wisdom;
and who now, with that great cloud of witnesses,
watches and cheers
as another mother runs her appointed race.

Contents

FOREWORD / 9

1. Motherhood: History and Hope / 13
2. Only One Is Perfect and He Is In You / 21
3. Helicopter Mom, You're Creating a Draft / 29
4. Keeping Up Appearances / 37
5. Claiming Your Own Identity / 49
6. When Both You and They Make Mistakes / 57
7. The Sound of Silence / 65
8. The No Meddling Zone / 73
9. Dealing With Dads / 81
10. Shedding the Skin of Guilt / 91
11. Shattering the Stereotypes / 99
12. Contentment In Christ / 107

APPENDIX 1: Voices that Vote / 113

APPENDIX 2: Reading Resources / 121

NOTES / 123

ACKNOWLEDGMENTS / 127

ABOUT THE AUTHOR / 129

Foreword

So many books, so little time—not only to read but also to write. I have had this book in my heart for a long time. It is not so much about parenting styles or techniques, but how to be a free woman in Christ and consequently raise children who are free, like you, to fail or succeed. It is about knowing the One who is the source of your strength; that you were not meant to carry the burden of either perfection or guilt, but to be totally dependent on God, your heavenly Parent.

During the years I was raising my three children, I tried to be super mom. Until my third child was eleven, I was a stay-at-home mother. I loved them desperately and wanted to do the best possible job. I gave it my all and thought that their total well-being was in my hands. Yes, I had a wonderful husband who was the father of these children, but that still did not alleviate my passion to be perfect or the subsequent gut-wrenching guilt when, of course, I failed.

In the ensuing years, I have learned how the experience and calling of motherhood were designed to be very different from what is accepted as normal, even in Christian circles. I hear young mothers today struggling under the same false premises that I did, and it is mainly to them that I address this book. I always abhorred the adage "God couldn't be everywhere, so He made mothers." This well-known saying calls God's omnipresence into question and unwittingly makes mothers the fourth person of the Trinity. It is with great delight

9

that I turn this saying on its head and show that the very opposite is true.

Mothers Can't Be Everywhere, but God Is is designed to be read on the go; it is what I call pot-stirring literature—necessary, nutritious nuggets for mothers who are busy raising children. Each chapter can stand on its own. Even if time and the demands of little ones dictate that you cannot get through one chapter at first reading, there are appetizers to whet your appetite and give you sustenance to carry on until you can sit down for the main course.

The main source of this guilt-free book is certainly not my own expertise or excellence, rather the revelation of the New Covenant truth, "I have been crucified with Christ; and it is no longer I who live, but it is Christ who lives in me. And the life I now live in the flesh I live by faith in the Son of God, who loved me and gave Himself for me."[1]

At whatever stage you are in raising your children, there is something here for you. The book is meant to be a source of enlightenment and encouragement to mothers with or without a partner; and, without exception, whenever I have shared the concept of this book, the response has been a resounding "Yes!"

It is my prayer that *Mothers Can't be Everywhere, But God Is* will help you see your heavenly Father as the mighty God He is. The God who runs the universe can take care of your children and loves them beyond the fiercest mother love. May you be filled with hope and joy as you trust God who wants you to live every aspect of your life—and mothering is no exception—from the life of Christ within as you walk in His rest. Did somebody say rest? Is that possible while taking care of toddlers or teens? Read on, discover how, and be blessed.

MOTHERS
CAN'T BE EVERYWHERE
BUT GOD IS

🌹 *A*PPETIZERS

❶ *Our culture has developed unrealistic and inaccurate expectations of mothers.*

❷ *You were not meant to be everything to and everywhere for your children.*

❸ *Only God, the I AM, is omnipotent (all-powerful) and omnipresent (always everywhere) and omniscient (all-knowing).*

1

Motherhood: History and Hope

I USED TO SQUIRM under Mother's Day sermons. With few exceptions, the exhortation would be about the "virtuous woman" described in Proverbs 31. But the preacher invariably omitted the scripture's powerful references to this woman's expertise and influence outside the home, instead giving a narrow interpretation that extolled her role only as a mother. Around this time, I would also hear that recurring theme:

"God could not be everywhere, so He made mothers."

I would leave church carrying a red carnation and the burden of believing that my responsibility was greater than God's in raising my children.

As I collected my clamoring kinder from the nursery and Sunday school classes, there was no spring in my step on those bright May mornings, only a stinging sense of unfairness. As I collapsed into my car, I was also collapsing under the yoke of unattainable perfection, and as I ground the gears, I was giving way under the burden of guilt.

Now that I am a grandmother, I can dare to utter such seemingly heretical thoughts. In keeping with the scriptural exhortation to older women to teach the younger, I venture to offer some alternative reflections on the noble calling of motherhood. I start by heralding the good news that you as a mother cannot be everywhere, but God most certainly is.

The Genesis of God-likeness

All of humankind has bought the original lie, that we shall be as gods.[1] That fateful day of rebellion by our first parents at the dawn of time initiated our state of independence. Instead of depending totally on our Creator we leapt headlong into the depths, clutching only a lie for a life raft. We act as if we are solely responsible for our own lives and, even more sinisterly, the lives of others. When we enter the realm of motherhood, we find ourselves in a prime position to fulfill a life weighty in works. In *Charlotte's Web*,[2] the altruistic spider who labored to lay her single, once-in-a-lifetime pouch of eggs and then died, is suggestive of the extent to which women can unnecessarily sacrifice themselves in the process of mothering if they forget their dependence on God.

Mother love is powerful; but is it always healthy? Love does indeed cover a multitude of sins;[3] but are they covered by my flawed, though well-intentioned love, or only by God's agape kind of love? Jewel, the mother in Bret Lott's novel of the same name, maintains throughout the story that if only she loved her little Down's Syndrome daughter enough she would get better. Sadly, her love was not enough. Her insistence on her misguided mission caused her to unwittingly neglect the rest of her family.[4]

What is commonly celebrated as mother love is sometimes, albeit unconsciously, quite toxic. This toxic love doesn't cover a multitude of sins, but it only covers over a crippling dysfunctionality that may result in some kind of pathology that later emerges in the children's lives, and that produces guilt and failure in the mother. Mothers often grapple with guilt that pins them down instead of embracing God's grace—a light and easy companion that lifts us to live out of His love alone.

Spurious Science

As if our raging independence wasn't enough burden for us mothers to carry, science and religion add more bulk to our load. Most of us are quite unaware of the extent to which historical influences and religious premises affect our views of motherhood. Our society has built its expectations of women on faulty and cracked foundations.

Charles Darwin's theory of evolution evokes from many Christians a hearty defense of the Genesis account of creation. But are you aware that Darwin's assumptions have affected the way we women view our roles in society? So-called enlightened science sows seeds of insecurity and spurious thinking into female minds regarding their role as mothers. In Darwin's *The Origin of the Species*, he asserts that we evolve through a process called natural selection, and that the survival of the species depends largely on mothers protecting their offspring from the hazards of the environment. This teaching reinforces the original lie of the tempter that "Ye shall be as gods." Mothers have bought into that lie, believing they have a god-like role.

Although we may not be explicitly aware of such claims, nonetheless we are the beneficiaries of a century and a half of such implicit misinformation.

Darwin's contemporary Herbert Spencer, a social philosopher, profoundly influenced his thinking and ours as well. We have all become familiar with Spencer's expression, "survival of the fittest." When he applied this aphorism to women, he was signifying that we were primarily engineered to bear children, and this function had arrested our evolution. Thus, he reasoned, higher education would be wasted on us. We were passive, non-competitive, and incapable of higher reasoning.[5]

Spencer's contemporary, the author George Eliot, challenged this assessment of women in her novel, *Adam Bede*. She used the voice of one of her characters, the old school master Mr. Bartle, to highlight Spencer's ludicrous views. "That's the way with those women—they've got no head-pieces to nourish, and so their food all runs either to fat or to brats."[6] The fat bit we know about! What is sad is that women have habitually chosen to wear the other equally unwanted weight, the restrictive confinement of limited goals.

Repressive Religion

Although there has been much enlightenment regarding women in the twentieth century, these theories have created stubborn societal stains that are tough to remove. Moreover, religion—which often interprets God's truth through the filter of the prevailing worldview—has taken the baton and perpetuated the myths of gender roles and motherhood. In the book *Women and the Future of the Family*, Mardi Keyes writes:

> The mistake conservatives often make is to absolutize what they call the "traditional" division of labor—man is the breadwinner and a woman's place is in the home raising children—as if God established and sanctioned that particular division of labor for all time. In fact, there is nothing particularly biblical or traditional about that division of labor. It was one way of coping with the upheaval of industrialization and the consequent removal of economic work from the home.[7]

The economics of agrarian societies counted on children, lots of them, both to work in the fields and provide for their aging parents. Thus, women were perpetually pregnant, weakened, and often died young. In such a culture, birth control and the subsequent liberation of women from these roles could have meant economic disaster.

Equally calamitous for us today are the largely misinterpreted passages of scripture regarding women's roles, despite the clarion clear, New Covenant cry, "There is no longer Jew or Greek, there is no longer slave or free, there is no longer male and female; for all of you are one in Christ Jesus."[8] What part of that don't we understand?

Our cramped comprehension of this truth traces its origin back to the Garden once more. One of the foundation stones of sexism is a misunderstanding of the pronouncements given by God to Adam and Eve after the Fall. This occurs through mistranslation and misinterpretation of the last part of the verse in Genesis 3:16 which reads, "and he shall rule over you." The Hebrew wording, supported by linguistic scholars in the Semitic languages, maintains that "will" should be used instead of "shall."[9] This then becomes *descriptive* of what would now occur due to the couple's disobedience, not—as it has been labored over the centuries—*prescriptive* of our fate forever. If a woman chooses to turn to man rather than God for her governorship, man will indeed become her ruler.

Another classic clamp on women's equality comes from one of the Apostle Paul's letters. These verses have often been shallowly, subtly, and spuriously interpreted and applied to keep us in our place. Paul wrote to Timothy, "…and Adam was not deceived, but the woman was deceived and became a transgressor. Yet she will be saved through childbearing, provided they continue in faith and love and holiness, with modesty" (1 Timothy 2:13-15). Despite the fact that most orthodoxy would, without hesitation, declare that there is only one way to be saved, through Christ Jesus, there lingers in some

Christian circles a hint that women may still need to do something more—just to be sure. No doubt this view gains credence because it is coupled with the deep and deadly charge that women are more readily deceived than men. "Being saved through childbirth" then can be seen as the additional antidote for the particular poison that women introduced into the sin system. No, the sin of neither mother nor child may be atoned by motherhood, but only by the blood of Christ.

For a full and flowing explanation, I refer you to Richard and Catherine Clark Kroeger's great book, *I Suffer Not a Woman*.[10] These veteran scholars, along with all balanced scholars of the scriptures, suggest that Galatians 3:28 promises that the mother's life will be preserved during or throughout childbirth. From the Greek verbs used in the text, the authors go on to bolster their case that the context of this section in Paul's letter to the Galatians refers to childbirth. It doesn't prescribe the conditions under which a woman gains acceptance into God's family.

Even if these arguments are "all Greek" to many mothers, the outworking of science and history's conclusions and biases certainly do color our views of mothering. I have just given a cursory glance at these bulwarks of thought. However, I hope it has helped to show how we may have bought a view of our status as women that hampers our freedom in Christ.

In the following chapters, we will look at various facets of our role and the difference it makes in our mothering when we live from God's life within us. This book does not present a formula nor guarantee success in child-rearing. It only presents the hope that we can become free women and raise free children who will in turn be at liberty to experience both success and failure and, in the process, learn to find the source of their strength solely in Christ.

Nourishing Nuggets from *The Message:*

"So if the Son sets you free, you are free through and through" (John 8).

"Christ has set us free to live a free life. So take your stand! Never again let anyone put a harness of slavery on you. I am emphatic about this" (Galatians 5).

🌹 APPETIZERS

❶ *Trying to be perfect is an all-consuming task that will leave you exhausted.*

❷ *If you are a Christian, then Christ is your source of energy and enthusiasm.*

❸ *Let Christ live His life through you and parent your children through you.*

2

Only One is Perfect and He Is In You

I AM THINKING right now of three mothers I have known. They had much in common during their child-rearing years. They were smart, conscientious, committed, and wanted more than anything else to raise their children in the nurture and admonition of the Lord. Whatever that meant, it certainly did not mean losing their cool and using expletives in interactions with their children! Yet, each one of these three mothers finally did just that when they reached levels of exasperation and frustration with their grown children. I was one of those mothers, and my son's response to my outburst was, "Now I see Mom as human after all." Another mother heard her son say in response to her tirade, "Now I've seen you as a person." The third, I believe, never quite caught his breath in time to respond to his mom's colorful convulsion!

Failure Reveals the Rock

What mother hasn't become exasperated and reacted in anger toward her children at some point? Although the reasons for a mother's outburst may vary—from simple frustration to the child's invasion of her boundaries—her over-reaction may leave her feeling like a failure. But such failures can have enduring and healthy results. It is good for both mother and child to appreciate that mom is human and that the only source of perfection is God. For moms, what a relief to relinquish the need to be perfect. When we apologize for our outbursts and for our failure to avail ourselves of the richness of the English language (rather than resort to common expletives), this serves to strengthen the familial bond and reciprocal respect.

I and many of my peer group have lived to see some of our grown children make choices that leave us winded, wounded, and wondering where in the world we went wrong. We stayed at home—no day care for our children; we sat with our families in the pews every time the church doors opened; the Word reigned supreme. How do we come to terms, then, with outcomes in our children's lives that indicate our best efforts may have failed?

Seismic events in the lives of my grown children shattered what remained of my belief that there was a formula for raising fail-proof children. But the good news is that as the ground heaved beneath my feet, the Rock was revealed. God revealed Christ. Although an ardent student of the Word, I finally had a revelation of what Jesus was getting at when He said, "You search the scriptures because you think that in them you have eternal life; and it is they that testify on My behalf. Yet you refuse to come to Me to have life" (John 5:39, 40).

I had missed the pertinent point that *He* is my perfection, my fail-proof life—not my own efforts, expertise, or religious zeal. Now I look back over my active mothering years and wish that I had known these truths then. I am grateful, though, that I now have the opportunity to mentor young mothers and the privilege of sharing these truths with mothers still in the process of raising and influencing their little ones.

In the book of Job, God describes Job as "perfect" or "complete." The original Hebrew word here comes from a root word which can be translated "to be spent, consumed." I believe Job was consumed and exhausted with trying to be righteous; with compensating for whatever sin his children might be indulging in; with maintaining and defending his reputation in the community. The quest for perfection consumed him. In a sense, our ancient brother Job was the quintessential mother. His wife seemed to have no such scruples about parenting or even her relationship with her Creator. In exasperation she exhorts her husband to "curse God and die" (Job 2:9). Like Job, and unlike his wife, many mothers struggle with perfectionism.

Author Kathy Collard Miller, in her great little book, *When Counting to 10 Isn't Enough*, writes:

> ...Megan, the mother of a fifteen month old, lives under the burden of an emotional dictator called perfectionism. Always striving to be better, she picks out and concentrates on her slightest error, even when her behavior is acceptable... It wasn't until Megan began to understand the difference between perfectionism and Christian perfection that she could accept herself as a person and as a child of God.[1]

The Myth of Perfectionism

That quest for the mythical Holy Grail of perfectionism is responsible for dumping more guilt on a mother's heart than anything else of which I am aware. We buy into the paradigm and, from the moment we know we are pregnant until our children graduate from high school and beyond, we assume a larger than necessary burden of responsibility for our child's welfare. While we do pray for help, we still can't quite shake the suspicion that God is sometimes disapproving of our performance. *After all*, we seem to reason, *He cannot be everywhere, and has left me personally in charge of this precious child.*

Holding a newborn infant in our arms is an awesome, glorious, and yet frightening experience. Babies arrive wrapped in the smell of heaven, which will soon be exchanged for the earthly redolence of throw-up and messy diapers. We feel completely responsible—only moms can feed them, particularly if we are breast-feeding; only moms may want, or know how, to change their diapers; and only moms seem to have the insight to know what is needed when everyone else resorts to handing back the inconsolable baby. No wonder a mom seems to think she is the god-person.

Brenda Hunter supports this popular assumption when she writes:

> No one can ever replace you in your children's lives. For them you are the sun, the moon, the whole universe. You are your children's only mother, and if you are too often absent, harried, or preoccupied, they may yearn for you all of their lives.[2]

While these are wonderful, and to a large extent, true sentiments, they serve only to heap more guilt on the mother who fails to measure up. Loss of a mother or mother figure is not a trifling issue. It is a tragedy and does leave a gaping hole in our lives but not one that is beyond repair. God clearly has promised that even if father and mother do forsake us, He will never abandon us.[3]

By contrast, consider the revelation that a friend shared with me recently.

> When I was first riding home from the hospital with my daughter I was pretty anxious," she said. "I remember putting my head back on the seat and clearly hearing Christ say, "Let me be the mother through you." That calmed me considerably.

Learning Christ as Life

Our heavenly Parent planned it this way. Paul writes in his letter to the Christians in Galatia that when God revealed Christ in him, he realized, "I have been crucified with Christ; and it is no longer I who live, but it is Christ who lives in me" (Galatians 2:19, 20). The God who only helps from afar is the God of the Old Covenant to whom the psalmist David cried. He recorded some of the most beautiful expressions of the human heart, yet his God was still a separate entity. In the New Covenant, He has come to dwell within the human heart. The mystery, hidden from the ages and of which the patriarchs longed to know, now revealed as "Christ in us the hope of glory" (Colossians 1:27). He no longer wants to simply help us from a distance; He wants to guide, nurture, encourage, stengthen, and enable us from the inside out.

Failures and frustrations on the outside squeeze us in order that the life of Christ may emanate from the inside, rather like the squeezing of a tube releases the toothpaste. The purpose of the container in the first place is to hold the contents of the tube. Our own weaknesses are blessings that reveal the bankruptcy of our own flesh to accomplish perfection. "The flesh" means the self-life, or attempting to live out of one's own resources. Some of us are more positively programmed than others, more naturally nice, of a pleasant and patient disposition—what we might call prime-cut flesh. Others are tougher, brasher personalities and could be considered analogous to chuck beef. It is all still flesh. Our first parents ate of the tree of the knowledge of both good and evil. Good is no more acceptable than evil in our relationship with God or in facilitating our freedom. His love is such that He will permit us to come to the end of our own good efforts in order to reveal the bankruptcy of the flesh, at which point we will be ready to exchange the self-life for the Christ-life.

So, the mother becomes the child, learning from her heavenly Parent even as she herself is parenting. The way to be free from the myth of being the perfect mother is to see that the only one who is perfect is Christ. We do not dispute that. What is hard to comprehend is that His perfect life has been imparted to us. Feel the tension diminish as we imagine really taking Jesus at His word, believing that we can do nothing without Him and trusting Him to parent through us—full of exquisite wisdom, love, and grace according to each child's particular needs and bent.

There is a story about a little girl who, on the way home from church, turned to her mother and said, "Mommy, the preacher's sermon this morning confused me."

The mother replied, "Oh! Why is that?"

"Well, he said God is bigger than we are. Is that true?"

"Yes, that is true."

"He also said that God lives within us. Is that true too?"

Again the mother replied, "Yes."

"Well," said the girl, "If God is bigger than we are, and He lives in us, wouldn't He show through?"[4]

Letting Him show through brings great relief. Our attempts to live separately from this indwelling life is an untenable position causing disappointment, dissonance, and depression in our own lives and certainly not what we want to impart to our beloved children. Our bottled-up frustration in failing to be perfect finally bursts through the thin veneer of pretense, resulting in more guilt and remorse over a less-than-perfect display of temper. Then the circle is complete.

Released Mom

I thought maybe I could make up for my less-than-perfect mother performance by being the perfect grandmother until I heard God say, "How are your grandchildren ever going to look for Me if you never let them down?" Every one of us, parent and child alike, must learn Christ for ourselves. As we learn to accept one another for who we are—as God accepts us—we are passing on the only perfection there is, His. As I said goodbye at the airport to my son and his wife recently, he leaned down to embrace me saying, "Thank you for loving us with God's love." I knew then that, by God's great grace, I had attained unto a new place of motherhood.

As this particular son and I have come to terms with one another's weaknesses, there is a far deeper, freer, richer bond between us. He is my son who is learning Christ's sufficiency in his life through his own failures. I am the mother who is willing to acknowledge that the good I strived for was not sufficient and that I must forgive myself for this.

In a touching moment in the movie, *Billy Elliot*, the dance teacher listens to descriptions of the boy's deceased mother, then says, "She must have been a special woman." To this Billy tersely replies in a broad, English North Country accent, "Na, she was just me mam!"[5]

At the end of the day, that is all we are, just moms. We are biologically blessed, emotionally ever involved, yet spiritually insufficient to the task without the indwelling life of Christ who is our perfection, a perfection that makes us right with both our God and our family. Let's celebrate the unique expressions of Christ that we are as women and mothers.

Nourishing Nuggets from *The Message:*

"When you're joined with me and I with you, the relation intimate and organic, the harvest is sure to be abundant. Separated, you can't produce a thing" (John 15).

"Whatever I have, wherever I am, I can make it through anything in the One who makes me who I am" (Philippians 4).

🌹 APPETIZERS

1 *If you hover to control every eventuality in your children's lives, you may blow them off the course that God has planned for them.*

2 *From the very beginning, you learn to let your children go.*

3 *From teething to toddling to teenage years, your children's heavenly Parent is in compassionate oversight of their lives.*

3

Helicopter Mom, You're Creating a Draft

I'M SURE THAT we are all familiar with news footage of dignitaries descending from a helicopter. They duck down and hold on to hat or hair until they are clear of the whirring blades of the helicopter that has deposited them at their destination. Only when they are safely out of the wind, can they stand upright, readjust their clothing and coiffures, and then proceed to their engagements.

Controlling for Take-Off

When my daughter was raising little ones, I first heard of the helicopter analogy. It paints a picture of a fussing, overly solicitous mom who is fearful to let Tommy toddler try anything new without the constant whirring of her benevolent blades. Then, just as the helicopter hovers over its occupants even after they have disembarked, so we often continue trying to control our children even when they are grown and gone, creating the kind of draft that causes our offspring to duck out of the way. The current is often so great that they feel helpless to be free of its influence—an influence that haunts them and continues to disturb their adult lives. If they do get away, they don't come back.

We hover because we think we can preside over all the

eventualities of our children's lives. Of course genuine, responsible guidance is essential, especially to ensure the physical welfare of a small child. But we often go beyond what's necessary, thinking that if only we stay near to oversee, then we will be able to make sure no evil befalls them. This propensity is yet another outward expression of our penchant for perfection. Our friend Job, whom we mentioned in the last chapter, forever offering sacrifices to atone for the possible sins of his sons and daughters, is also a great example of hovering to control all eventualities. The record shows that in Job's family God had a far-reaching plan that included grave loss and tragedy before eventually, good prevailed.

We are often unaware that the draft we cause with our fussing actually blows our children off course and out of the wind of the Spirit who is directing their lives. Someone once compiled a list of a few examples of how our natural proclivities as mothers sometimes get in the way of the greater good:

- Being a mother is wanting to pick up your children each time they fall, but teaching them to pick themselves up instead.

- Being a mother is wanting to keep them from all hurt and harm, but knowing that they must be taught to take care of themselves.

- Being a mother is wanting to give them the best of everything, but knowing they will value life more if they wait and work for many of their rewards.

My own rewarding mothering life is replete with illustrations of yours truly as Helicopter Mom. Many years ago, one of our sons was living alone some distance from us, where he was working just before going to college. From every communication I had with him, it appeared that his life was one catastrophe after another. Following one telephone conversation, I slumped down into the chair saying, "God, please do something."

The response was swift and searing: "I will, if you get out of the way!"

I was dumbfounded. God could do it!—without my fretting, cajoling, or even sending care packages. And He did. In the heavenly Parent's own good time, all the issues were resolved—car finally up and running, rent money provided, fingers healed from a nasty accident—and my son took another step on the journey of trusting the God who is everywhere, rather than a mother who is not.

Heavenly Parentage Does Not Hover

As much as we care, think about how little control we have when our babies are forming in the womb. Though we can exercise and eat right, we cannot determine their personality, the color of their hair, eyes, or even their gender—despite a plethora of folksy methods suggested to guarantee a boy or a girl. Even with the rapidly approaching specter of human cloning crossing our horizon (which sounds like heaven for control addicts), God alone holds the life force in His hands. Even if science and questionable ethics collude in forming a human being, surely that life will still exist beyond our ability to dictate its destiny. The heavenly Parent is the one who designates the journey.

From the moment we first hold our babies in our arms, we need to grasp this holy concept: God has paths planned for them from the foundation of the earth. In the case of the little lives whose destinies are snuffed out before they begin, the Father still has the final say. When mothers use the ultimate means of control by aborting their unborn babies, I believe that these lives return to His presence and fulfill His purposes in another realm (See 2 Samuel 12:22, 23).

Whether at the far end of the spectrum as in abortion, or at any point along the continuum of parental choices, the need to control has its roots firmly embedded in fear. The presence of fear means we are unaware of the intensity of God's love and care for us. Fear drives us to take matters into our own hands. A quote from a mother in a recently-published book labels it accurately, "The worst thing about being a mother is not the sleepless nights or dirty diapers or less money or whatever. It's just the fear. I don't know how to keep both of them safe every second of the day!"[1] We do not have to know how; we only need to know the One who can and does.

An insightful and wise friend has suggested that in the same way men find it hard to let God be God in their work, women find it hard to let God be God in their children's lives. Pronouncements from the pulpit frequently support the stance of the parent's sole responsibility in child rearing. I recently watched a TV preacher pacing the platform cradling a baby in his arms and declaring that parents are wholly responsible for their child's future behavior, citing the infamous Colorado Columbine High School shooting in 1999 where two students ran amok killing classmates and a teacher. He bellowed, "Who lit the fuse on their time bomb? You, the parent did."

While there is much that parents do to influence their children for good or evil, the decisions children make are ultimately theirs alone, especially in the decision to accept or reject Christ as Savior. A friend of mine writhed under a burden of guilt regarding her children's spiritual destiny after she heard her pastor pronounce that it was her responsibility to get that child through the pearly gates.

Thanks be to God that we are not the ultimate authority in the lives of our progeny. He has provided from His rich repository for both their present and their future. Four years ago one of my precious grandbabies was born, just three months after my father's death. He had died thousands of miles from where his fourth great-grandchild came into the world. Apart from the obvious bloodlines, they had something else in common: angels. As I looked at my father's still and cold form that May morning, I ached that he had died alone in his little cottage in his native Scottish islands. Then it seemed I heard the Father say, "He was not alone. My angel brought him home." When I later gazed in rapture at the warm bundle of new life, I knew this child had not arrived alone either. Angels had come with him and would watch over him until he left this earth.

In Matthew 18:10, the gospel writer indicates that the angels in charge of the children ever look toward God the Father for their instructions. I've always found it significant and immensely comforting that they are looking to the Father, not to their charges or their mothers.

Limits of Loving and Praying

Well, if hovering and controlling is out for mothers, then what about prayer? Surely prayer is a more effective and safe domain for the concerned mother. I had an epiphany regarding even the parameters of prayer once. My son and his fiancée had given me a date when they were en route to a certain destination, so I ensconced myself to pray during the hours of the journey, being careful to adjust for time zones. I discovered some days later that they had changed the date (without telling me!) and had traveled a few days earlier, and without my prayer covering.

Not only that, but they had been involved in a serious rollover in their old pick-up truck and yet had escaped unscathed. I was compelled to conclude that their heavenly Parent could bring them through without my accompanying prayer, though I like to believe that perhaps He responded retroactively in this case!

Please understand, I fervently believe in prayer. I'm not entirely clear as to how it works, only that it does and is often my only recourse, the only thing I can do in most situations. However, this story illustrates the fact that God cares more than any mother can and is consistently committed to our children's welfare and training. Heavy and aching mother hearts find access to a kind of prayer that intercedes perfectly and accurately; groanings of the spirit that are beyond words, or "too deep for words" (Romans 8:26).

Our love motivates us to want the best for our priceless children, and our love is undisputedly powerful. Yet, as I stood under the hot Phoenix sun some years ago and viewed the quilt created to commemorate the victims of AIDS on its nationwide tour, one sentiment among the many thousands of hand-designed epitaphs stood out. It simply said, "If love could have kept you, you never would have died."

Our love is limited and lacks the divine perspective. As such, our attempts to control can result in over-involvement in our children's lives that ranges from the ridiculous, like the mother who wanted to go on her daughter's honeymoon, to the more sinister situation of the son who felt constrained to call his mother when sexual temptation with his fiancée threatened to overtake him. Such was the extent of the toxicity in that unhealthy mother-son relationship. Kenneth M. Adams poses a piercing question for our consideration:

> Did you have a parent whose love for you felt more confining than freeing, more demanding than giving, more intrusive than nurturing?[2]

Yes, we are in a wonderfully privileged position, and we may well be our child's best, and most trusted, friend. We do have the responsibility to be available to listen, guide, and model, but our best efforts cannot preside over every outcome. Our calling is simply to stand, confident of the supremacy of God as their perfect Parent. If we stand still, we do not create unwanted currents.

We do the best by our children when we cultivate calmness and model faith instead of fretting and manipulating. As we learn to relinquish our need for control, we are free to love more unconditionally and lend support, rather than running to the rescue. When we allow our children, no matter how little they are, to take responsibility for their own behaviors, we facilitate the flow of health, wholeness, and wisdom in their lives. Dorothy Canfield Fisher, an eighteenth-century writer, rightly said, "A mother is not a person to lean on, but a person to make leaning unnecessary."[3]

Let's start early to lift off in our helicopters so our children can run clear of the whirring blades and have the opportunity to know only the wind of God's Spirit as their guiding force.

Nourishing Nuggets from *The Message:*

"You realize, don't you, that their personal angels are constantly in touch with my Father in heaven?" (Matthew 18).

"Don't fret or worry. Instead of worrying, pray. Let petitions and praises shape your worries into prayers, letting God know your concerns. Before you know it, a sense of God's wholeness, everything coming together for good, will come and settle you down. It's wonderful what happens when Christ displaces worry at the center of your life" (Philippians 4).

🌹 *A*PPETIZERS

❶ *Pushing for performance may mean you do not understand your child's unique wiring.*

❷ *The seeds of the "disease to please" are sown in childhood.*

4

Keeping Up Appearances

A BRITISH COMEDY series called *Keeping Up Appearances*[1] fea-
tures Hyacinth, a pretentious, middle-aged lady who spends her
entire life giving the impression of status, wealth, and influence
to whomever she deems worthy to impress. This is of more
importance to her than identifying with her renegade, lower-
class relatives. It is funny and, as with most humor, causes us
to laugh because we at some level can identify. Who of us, like
Hyacinth, has not wanted to distance ourselves from embarrass-
ing or disappointing family members who offend our cultivated
sensibilities, or who has not tried to give the impression that
we have it all together as a family—our marriage zings, and our
children are perfect?

Pushing for Performance

Mothers who project the image of mythical perfection will
try to perpetuate that image in their children as well. That will
mean pushing for performance, frequently producing children
who are not free to be who God created them to be. Much of
this activity comes from us mothers trying to live vicariously
through our children or comparing them to their peers, their
cousins, or the neighbors' kids. In her book, *The Drama of the
Gifted Child*, Alice Miller presents the theory that a mother is
largely responsible for the emotional problems of her children

and may use her children to fulfill her own needs instead of meeting the needs of the children. The child will then act as the mother wants.[2] Thus, the cycle of keeping up appearances runs on into another generation.

Disappointment in our child's performance may have its genesis in our failure to understand his or her natural predispositions; the unique potential with which each child comes into the world.

All my life I have wanted to do what I am now doing, writing. But, because of the economic and social climate of the time in which I lived, as a young person my options were limited in choosing a career path. Out of the three popular possibilities—teacher, secretary, or nurse—I chose the last. Many times throughout my nursing life, I would find myself gazing at the large Georgian façades of the major newspaper houses in the city of Edinburgh, aching to be rushing to meet deadlines rather than bustling with bedpans. (As I complete my second book, I thank God that it is never too late to pursue what we are created to do, for He is faithful and nothing can thwart His purposes.)

It is not our job to decide, create, or carve out our children's gifts and talents, but to guide them according to their bent (See Proverbs 22:6). Only by the time our third child came along, did my husband and I understand this. Catching on to his wiring, we were able to encourage his individual natural talents. Parental guiding is about natural talents as much as it is about spiritual training.

We find our offspring's traits and tendencies by relinquishing our own expectations, aspirations, and plans. Then God can show us who this amazing person is whom He has entrusted to our care. Then we discover that he may not want to inherit the family business, go to our alma mater, or try out for the football team. If we are convinced of our custodial role and not our omniscient one, it is an exciting adventure to watch God develop His creation. It is a great joy to be a partner in the divine plan of the ages instead of maneuvering and manipulating and then reaping the harvest of a frustrated and perhaps bitter and resentful child. We all know young women and men who agonize over their career choices, wondering why in the world they feel so out of place. Many times they conclude, and rightly, that they are there because parents did not know how to elicit their divine destiny.

A close cousin to "keeping up appearances" is "the curse of comparisons." If we succumb to comparing one child to another, not only do we frustrate their individual endowments, but we also set up rivalries between the siblings that can develop into full-blown enmity in the future. (You may have noticed that not much help is required to set siblings against one another, for they already come with that legacy of rivalry and squabbling inherited from the first pair of sibs, Cain and Abel.)

Most of us moms are probably too perceptive and spiritually sensitive to engage in any of these destructive behaviors consciously. However, unwittingly, we can readily let an attitude, a look, or a withdrawal of approval speak volumes about either our disapproval or our favor. Compare this: When you relate stories about each child, does one receive more accolades than the other? Which one has the most works of art on the refrigerator door? It is a fact that we may find one of our children easier to get along with simply because of a more natural match due to personality affinity. We need not be embarrassed over this, only recognize that we will need to lean more heavily on the life of Christ within not to either show favoritism or be unduly critical of their siblings.

At the far end of the spectrum, experts tell us that child abuse grows out of the wish of the parent to project the child as an extension of his or her own identity. If the child misbehaves or fails to perform, it is seen as a slight to the parent's ego; it dashes the parent's expectations and attempts to gain other people's approval. The child's failure to perform to mother's standards further erodes her poor self-image, causing mother to lash out at her child in misdirected frustration and anger.

A Gift, or a Grief

If you have been given gifted children to care for, then there will be less need to impress, although surprisingly, there is always somebody smarter, more athletic, and more beautiful. We have only to peek at the world of pageants and sports to see the results of exploiting our children's gifting. Blessedly, the extremes, as showcased in the tragic, unsolved murder of the young Colorado girl Jon Benet Ramsey in 1997, are rare but serve to highlight the dangerous waters into which parents can launch their gifted child in the race to win.

A good friend back in England told me of the shock her son encountered when he went off to prep school thinking he was the smartest boy in the country only to discover he was but one of many. If your child is clever, then rejoice, channel the energies, and know they stand in their own silver socket, not reflecting you. One of the many insightful, dedicated mothers whom I interviewed gave a graphic illustration of this when she described how the Lord made her aware that she was wearing her sons as ornaments around her neck.[3] She described her journey to jettisoning this weight as "a journey I would repeat over and over to know my God as the all-sufficient heavenly Parent."

The converse is also true. Just as your gifted child does not owe his or her success to you, neither does your challenged little one reflect your failure. In both cases, we need the wisdom and patience of Christ to guide and tap each unique life. Whether your child is challenged mentally, emotionally, or physically, you can be comforted in knowing that your Father makes no mistakes in His assignments.

Someone gave me an article that the late Erma Bombeck had written on God's choice of mothers. "Here is a woman whom I will bless with a child less than perfect. She does not know it yet, but she is to be envied."[4] Such a mother, feeling somewhat less than enviable, recently recounted her utter exasperation and bone-grinding weariness in dealing with her challenged child. "God, why did you give this child to me?" Then she realized with comforting clarity that He had not given her this little one because she could manage, but because she could not manage without her God. My daughter is that blessed mother; and I am the blessed grandmother.

In a discussion at my book club the other night, various opinions surfaced regarding the viability and validity of the lives of severely handicapped children. One group member felt that by electing to preserve the life of such a child, the life of the parent would be radically ruined. To this I replied, "So-called normal children can equally ruin your life through the choices they make."

If we feel that any of our children have "ruined" our lives, whether by their choices or their debilities, it is tempting to succumb to feelings of shame. The rewards of resisting reproach and embracing unconditional love toward them are immeasurable. Children who experience acceptance, and are valued for who they are and not for their performance, are less likely to grow up crippled with a yoke of shame themselves.

We are not responsible for the arrival of either the gifted or the challenged child, only for letting God be the Parent through us, as He delights in His choice of us as the mother.

When we get free of the need to make the "right impression" or to look good to others (who really are not as interested in our lives as we think they are, or we consider they ought to be), then our children also will be free to become who they are.

A faulty element in the Christian ethos, and it certainly was in mine, is in the way we often suppress and do not permit our children to express anger because we consider it a carnal indulgence that does not reflect Christ. Suppressing a legitimate, God-given emotion presages grave consequences for the future. Repressed anger will almost certainly manifest in self-destructive behavior in adulthood. The overriding need to present the "Waltonian" family image at the expense of freedom of expression is dangerous, and once more shows us that we do not understand the unconditional love of our God who has made us acceptable in the Son, entirely independent of our performance.

The Possibilities of the Prodigal

No chapter on keeping up appearances would be complete without the greatest performance buster of all, the prodigal. If there was ever a situation that pours self-recrimination, regret, and remorse on a mother, it is this one. Whether or not we may have contributed to the child leaving home, faith, church, and even in some cases, God, our child has made a decision that we must respect; we must not chide ourselves over our children's autonomous choices.

Although mention of the mother is missing in the most famous account of a prodigal as told by Luke in chapter fifteen of his gospel, there can be little dispute that she is there. Henri Nouwen's riveting book, *The Return of the Prodigal Son*, was inspired by a long and penetrating study of Rembrandt's painting of this story. He sees the mother in the hands of the father:

The father's left hand touching the son's shoulder is

strong and muscular. How different is the father's right hand! It lies gently upon the son's shoulder—to offer consolation and comfort. It is a mother's hand.[5]

Just as the parents in the parable wait, we too wait—ready to celebrate our prodigal's return without retribution. One mother admitted that it was easier for her husband to accept their daughter's return than it was for her. Her question exemplifies the unrealistic mantle that a mother assumes for the destiny of her child. "What will people say about me as a mother?"

The prodigal passage may represent one of the hardest trials of a mother's heart. But, after we have cried an ocean and wailed into the dark silence of the night, hope will come in on the morning tide. Hope in God. He is the heavenly Parent and is willing to wait, knowing that we all must come to an end of our own self-sufficiency before we become truly dependent on Him and not ourselves. Let the prodigal process have its way. It is far more important for your wandering child to find the Father, than for him to make you look good. Note an interesting fact from the narrative in Luke. As the prodigal rehearses his speech in contemplation of returning to his father, he concludes that he is no longer worthy to be called his father's son. Only the welcome home would convince him that his sonship was not based on his behavior. He was a son because he was from his father's seed.

Henri Nouwen says that we are all prodigals if we are looking for our approval and acceptance from anywhere other than God.[6] That includes mothers. Are we looking for the commendation of the church, family, or community that we want to impress with our perfect family, while our prodigal causes us shame and embarrassment? Then we too are being profligate in terms of our relationship with our heavenly Father, since we are looking for our identity outside of Christ. When our selfhood is

43

extricated from that of our child's, then we are unashamed and liberated to love enough to let them go. We can let our reputation slip and learn our own utter dependence on God while we wait for them to learn it as well.

Harking back to Hyacinth for a moment. In occasional episodes, she is heard talking on the telephone to her son Sheridan, and she then goes to great lengths to explain away his aberrant activities in an attempt to deflect any suspicion that he may be gay. Coming to terms with a child who is homosexual threatens our Christian reputation big time. I remember the thinly veiled sorrow when it was a friend's turn to share about her family during an intimate dinner party. After lauding her daughter she arrived at her son and with equal pride, but with tears said, "He is a successful businessman, and he is gay. We love and totally accept him."

Being a Christian mom is no safeguard against our child choosing an alternative life style. Accepting, integrating, and coming to terms with it will drive us to dependency on God's resources like few other events we may encounter. This is what a friend said regarding her experience with her lesbian daughter: "It has taken knowing who I am in Christ to bring me out and through."

Sowing the Seeds of Freedom

"Out and through" offers the way to freedom from the bondage of seeking external approval. The more we learn this as young mothers, the sooner our little ones will too, and thereby we will inoculate them against the seeds of the "disease to please" which starts in childhood. Teaching them how to protect their own divinely-built boundaries is as important as having their shots against physical diseases.

While still in diapers, my little granddaughter gave a perfect illustration of how boundaries work. She clearly recognized the line of demarcation between where she ended and her offending diaper began. When one of her siblings told her that she stunk, she immediately replied. "I don't stink, my diaper stinks." It is imperative that we, while teaching our little ones the power and privilege of faith, remind them that their boundaries, their sovereignty of selfhood, is a sacred place that they must guard. These boundaries are wide open to invasion if our children are unaware that they have needs of their own. This is the whole principle of the Body of Christ—interdependency. Yet too often Christian children grow up fed only with their obligation to give. If their emotional diet is deficient in the essential element of *receiving*, our children will choose from a smorgasbord of toxic relationships in the future, liaisons that will leach their strength while giving them nothing in return.

Children arrive in this world with a disarming honesty that fails the test of political-correctness. In an engaging little book called *From the Lips of Children*, Richard Wurmbrand offers this illustration:

> When Mrs. Booth of the Salvation Army preached on one occasion, she noticed a child in the front row crying. She paused to comment, "I am moved to see a child weeping at the sufferings of Jesus." An adult might have been happy to accept the compliment. But the child stood up and admitted, "No, lady, an insect got into my eye." Let us not pretend to have more spirituality than we actually possess.[7]

We have no need to pretend in order to gain either the approval of God or man. We have no need to hide our pain or the less than perfect places and people in our lives. I am always moved by the record of the great Apostle Paul who never hid the names and the deeds of those of his circle who had brought him hurt or shame. He saw they were God's responsibility, and his candor empowers us to be honest with our lives without detracting from our worth and reputation.[8] Our worth is forever secure in the Father's eyes, as is our children's. Striving to please and impress is unnecessary and futile, for we are unable to please all of the people all of the time, ever! What relief and joy to revel in the unwavering approval of God alone who does not judge by outward appearances, but sees our inner person, reborn and indwelt by the crucified and resurrected life of Christ.

Nourishing Nugget from *The Message:*

"Have some of you noticed that we are not yet perfect? My ego is no longer central. It is no longer important that I appear righteous before you or have your good opinion, and I am no longer driven to impress God. Christ lives in me. The life you see me living is not 'mine,' but it is lived by faith in the Son of God, who loved me and gave Himself for me. I am not going to go back on that" (Galatians 2).

🌹 APPETIZERS

1 *The great work (magnum opus) of your life is not raising your children, but becoming like Christ.*

2 *You may know who you are as a wife, mother, lover, employee, or employer. But, who are you as a person?*

5

Claiming
Your Own Identity

SHE STANDS in the middle of her trophies—her family room replete with portraits: the "Sears' specials" of her children at every birthday up until age five; thereafter the grinning award acceptance pictures snapped at school and church; the photos that capture happy camping days, roasting weenies and s'mores; then the graduation and wedding pictures. Susan looks around at all that remains of her children in her now spotless home and asks, "What now, Lord?"

It is no rhetorical question. Like thousands of mothers who have devoted themselves exclusively to taking care of their families, she wonders what to do now that they are gone. More importantly, she wonders who she is. Susan continues, "I feel like I lost myself in the process."

The Confusion of Calls

Such an all-eclipsing process is child-raising. It is all too easy to forget to claim ourselves in this period of our lives, and even if we vaguely recall something about our own individual identity, we find little time to excavate it. However, this search for ourselves is an imperative pursuit. The more we realize who we are as persons, the more fulfilled, content, and competent we will be as mothers.

I first arrived in the U.S.A. from Scotland in the late sixties when the stampede of women who were charging to get outside the home and be "more fulfilled" was starting. A neighbor asked me, "What do you do?" When I responded that I was a wife and mother, she then probed further, "I mean, what do you really do?" The information that I was a nurse by profession prompted the enquirer to excitedly explain that there was a great demand for nurses and I would readily secure a position. My smug, Old World response usually curtailed the conversation. "The world can get plenty of nurses, but my children have only one mother."

Danielle Crittenden in her book *What Our Mothers Didn't Tell Us* explores the failure of feminism:

> If previous generations of women were raised to believe that they could only realize themselves within the roles of wife and mother, now the opposite is thought true: It's only outside these roles that we are able to realize our full potential and worth as human beings. Once a husband and children were thought to be essential to a woman's identity; today, they are seen as peripherals, accessories that we attach only after our full identities are up and running. And how are we supposed to create these identities?[1]

I was able to be a stay-at-home mom, and it was in this role that I found my identity. When I was nursing, that was my selfhood. Many years later when my children were long gone, I was in Christian ministry and during that phase, my identity was as a woman minister. No matter what it is we are doing, we rarely see beyond that position as defining who we really are. Cult figures like the pop star Madonna, whose self-indulgence and pursuit of fame and adulation is considerable, now declare that all success fades into insignificance in the light of motherhood. As good as that sounds, it is still not the ultimate plan for our lives.

Cultivating an identity out of what we do is cheating ourselves. It implies that we are awaiting completion in something we accomplish, rather than God's intention of completing us in simply being—being in Christ, that is.

Despite multiple accomplishments, opportunities and recognition, many women still feel a gnawing sense of something missing. I like the way the author Sarah Ban Breathnach describes this longing in her book, *Something More*:

> Our insatiable, inexplicable longing probes the emptiness much the same way you do when you can't keep your tongue out of the sensitive, empty spot that once held a decaying tooth.[2]

The search to find, and fill up, what seems to be lacking leads in an ongoing search that steers us ever farther away from the Source that is within. If we are honest, we will admit that even we Christian mothers can be heard crying out, "Who am I, Lord?"

The Call of Christ Within

We do not have to go out there to search for something more. Our treasure is inside. These majestic words describe the New Covenant: "For in Him dwells all the fullness of the Godhead bodily; and you are complete in Him, who is the head of all principality and power" (Colossians 2:9,10 NKJV).

We are complete in Christ. That means that even if I am never a mother, never have a fulfilling occupation, or never attain to a prominent profession, in Christ Jesus I am entire and undiminished. How good of God to define us according to our intrinsic self, not our external attributes, achievements, or associations.

The revelation of what it means to be *in Christ* is a journey of increasing freedom and joy. Our God is a very practical Parent, and His purposes are neither esoteric nor arbitrary, but motivated by love for our highest good. He knows that if our bottom line identity is in His Son, we will never be disappointed. The career we craved and carved out will fall prey to the vagaries of the marketplace—without our permission; the top post in our profession will exact a price in time and energy that will leave us exhausted and disillusioned. Motherhood, despite its joys and fulfillment, involves wills other than our own, and our attempts to control all eventualities are doomed to failure. What we thought would be the pinnacle of our life's work can sometimes bring an unfathomable depth of disappointment. Hear the words of a devoted, but deeply aggrieved mother and dear friend of mine. "Summer of '86. Sixteen years of our family's life wiped out in one bold statement: 'I'm leaving you.' ...Our daughter—loved, attractive, bold, and defiant—wanted no more of us."

As a line in an old hymn says, "He is not a disappointment." The unchanging, eternal, undiminished life that is the essential "I" is the Christ that lives within us.[3] As an adult living temporarily in Germany and in the painful process of learning German, I found prepositions taking on a completely new importance as I tried to speak the language accurately. But at no time are those little words more vital than in this familiar verse of scripture. He now lives *in* me and does not merely walk *with* me or even carry me when the going gets rough—as the sentiments that the anonymous poet in the otherwise beautiful poem, "Footsteps," implies—but He is *in* me to the very end.

That life within cannot disappoint either our God or us. It is unthreatened throughout the care-giving days of children at home, and it continues to stand secure long after they are gone. The Holy Spirit knows that the purpose of God is to complete the work He has begun in us, to awaken us to our real selves. The real you and the real me are new creations in Christ, totally identified with His death and resurrection and completely dependent on His life.

In my child-rearing days, the book *Fascinating Woman-hood*, by Helen Andelin,[4] was one of the texts used in teaching seminars across the country that attempted to quantify the feminine soul. It taught what is still at the core of much of the recycled material we hear in the church today: that women are subordinate to men; they have narrow, specific roles, and their responsibilities are best fulfilled in being wives and mothers.

All the way home from one of those sessions, I wept with frustration and cried to my God asking why He had ordered it so when my whole being revolted at such a prospect. I intuitively knew that this was not how I was to be fulfilled as a person. I was to cry a similar prayer many years later when in ministry: "Why have you put all this passion in me only to sublimate it to the rule of man?" All the time my Father's answer was in my heart. He had initiated the heart cry so that He could show me that my measure was not in gender, but in God.

If you are still raising your little ones, this is the optimum time for you to claim your own personhood. When I say "time," I am not suggesting you take hours away from your children to attend self-awareness conferences or self-actualizing workshops. If you occasionally have such opportunities then take advantage of them, of course. What I am advocating is to attend to the dissonance—do not dismiss it as discontent, and do not put on your guilt shirt. One of the roles of the Holy Spirit is to teach us who and where Christ is. He will persist in cutting through all the traditions and expectations until He reveals to us truth in Christ alone.[5]

Identity with Limitless Boundaries

In her attempt to find her real self, Joan Anderson wrote in her moving memoir *A Year by the Sea* that life is a work in progress, as ever-changing as a sandy shoreline along the beach. As a loving wife and supportive mother, she had slowly and unconsciously replaced her own dreams with the needs of her family. She had neglected to nurture herself and, worse, failed to envision fulfilling goals for her future.[6]

Our lives have limitless boundaries in the God of the universe. Cultivate listening to His still small voice. Be willing to give it precedence over the clamor and cacophony of creed, crowd, or current teaching. The voice of the Holy Spirit will reveal Christ as the source of power we need to live the full, authentic life that includes how to be the best kind of mother, a free woman raising free children. That freedom will ignite in our hearts when we turn to a serious, open-minded study of the Epistles, particularly Galatians, Ephesians, and Colossians. These come from the pen of Paul, to whom was given the gospel of grace of the indwelling Christ. This is not just an exercise that will benefit us, but as we see God's plan for the ages, our actions, behaviors, and attitudes will model the life of Christ to our children.

Our identity is not in them, and theirs is not in us. They will never be as interested in our lives as we are, and ever will be, in theirs. That is the nature of things. In fact, the more secure we are in our own identity, the less our grown children will feel obligated to create a life that has to include our interests or cater to our happiness. At the end of the day, we will only have to give account for our own lives and what we have done with the talents and gifts God gave us. Our children are not our talents. Our children are His.

When our little ones have gone to find the paths God has prepared for them from the foundation of the earth, we will find ourselves alone but not lonely, missing them but not immobilized. Rather, we will be on tiptoe with eager anticipation for the answer to the question, "What now, Lord?" The tenor of our days will not be determined by the tone of our grown children's phone calls. Unlike a hiking acquaintance of mine who once said on a trek in the Colorado high country, "My day is only a good day if my kids are okay." Instead, the Father has declared that every day is a good day when we know our trophy is Christ alone, regardless of the landscape of our children's lives.

Nourishing Nuggets from *The Message:*

"It is in Christ that we find out who we are and what we are living for" (Ephesians 1).

"Your old life is dead. Your new life, which is your real life—even though invisible to spectators—is with Christ in God. He is your life" (Colossians 3).

APPETIZERS

1 *Can you believe that sin "shall be no shame, but honor"?*

2 *God works all things together for good.*

3 *Freedom to choose is your God-given right. Allow your children that right too.*

6

When Both You and They Make Mistakes

MEMORABLE MOMENTS often occur in the most mundane of places—in the bathroom, washing the windows, or as in this instance, pumping gas. At a 7-Eleven many years ago, my pre-teen daughter ducked her head out of the car window and popped me a profound question. "What would you say if I came home pregnant?"

I was glad for the pump to hang on to and the exercise of filling the tank to divert my eyes. Because she was too young to be sexually active, I did not faint at that particular prospect. However, this was the moment that I knew would eventually come, so I said, "Well my darling, not much... because that's what I did." That pubescent little girl was once the precious baby I had carried as an unwed mother.

Sin Forgiven—Not Shame, but Honor

It was time for me to share a major mistake I had made in my youth, which she accepted without comment. There would be plenty of time to talk about the deeper ramifications. There is never a text book time or place to share these kinds of things, but when the question is asked, it should be answered appropriately, according to the child's level of understanding. At the gas pump, I had a choice to deny the truth, dodge the question, or in terror of the same thing happening to her, lay down the law and so strengthen the sin principle.[1] I'm so glad that I did not lose the opportunity to show the grace and goodness of a God who redeems every circumstance.

One of the most frequently quoted verses of Christian consolation is:

> We know that all things work together for good for those who love God, who are called according to His purpose (Romans 8:28).

This is also one of the least believed, acted-upon, and rested-in verses of the Bible. I know—particularly when our own deliberate sin is the cause of the pain. If we read on in Romans chapter eight, we will see that the purpose of all things working together for good is that we be conformed to the image of Christ.

There is a snag, though. We have to let Him define the good to which the text refers. When we relinquish our narrow interpretation (which usually means unperturbed tranquility, thank you very much), we will echo the words of Joseph in the Old Testament who, when he finally met up again with the brothers who had sold him into slavery, could say, "You meant it for evil, but God meant it for good." The boy with the many-colored coat had now become a ruler in Egypt.[2]

God's ability to turn our darkest moments into good tells me that He is God and I am not. Julian of Norwich, the fourteenth-century mystic wrote, "Though the soul's wounds heal, the scars remain. God sees them not as blemishes but as honors."[3]

After years of hiding my soul's scars, it was such an utter relief and joy to relinquish the protection of my own reputation. In all the years that I ministered to women, I only rarely and selectively offered full disclosure, for fear that others would think less of me. My righteousness was in my works, not in Christ.

A close friend shared with me a few years ago that when her son was getting married and would then gain possession of his birth certificate, her husband, the father, wanted to somehow have the young man's birth certificate changed to reflect a full nine months from their marriage until the date of the boy's birth. This saddened her for it spoke much more about her husband's lack of confidence in a God of forgiveness and restoration than about hiding timelines from a son conceived out of wedlock. Chances are pretty high that their son had already figured it out anyway.

Perfect Strength in Weakness

Weakness is anathema to the human mind-set. Regrettably, its presence is not too welcome in the church either, a place where our frailties should be shared and indeed rejoiced over.[4] We rejoice over the fact that our failings provide the opportunity to let Christ's life be our sufficiency.

So long as we as mothers (or fathers!) have not forgiven ourselves for our past misdeeds and infractions of either the laws of God or man, we'll certainly never be able to fully forgive our children for their blunders.

This truth applies to the mess we may have made of the present as well as the past. If today we succumbed to screaming, lost control of our temper, or over-disciplined our child due to frustration or weakness or both, we need forgiveness. It flows freely for our failures—from God's throne, and also from the hearts of our little children.

I can still see the big blue eyes and feel the chubby arms that squeezed my neck on the occasions that I would weep by the bedside of my little ones asking their forgiveness for my unjust actions of the day.

Our tears melded together and, as I confessed my sin, I was absolved by the tender voice whispering, "It's all right Mommy. I love you and forgive you."

In our ignorance of the process by which our heavenly Parent brings us into dependency on Him, we fail to see that He allows our sin to surface so that we will dive into His supply, the indwelling Christ. Too often, adversity is seen as a punitive punishment from a merciless God, a lack of faith, or as Satan getting after us. We can find ourselves rebuking the devil when all the time it is God who is working through our weakness to bring us to the end of ourselves.

Then all too often, we simply sweep our susceptibilities out of sight in order to display our supposed perfection. How many of us have ever hustled everybody into church on a Sunday morning, big Bible tucked under our arm, a gospel grin fixed on our face, when only minutes before, unholy war raged in the confines of the car? When fellow church-goers ask, "How are you?" our need to present ourselves as perfect will not permit us to respond with anything but "Great! Praise God!" The truth that we are in domestic conflagration would not be an acceptable answer. No matter how strong, skilled, or resourceful our natural life, though, it has to be exchanged for supernatural life. To operate in God's wisdom, we must first die to our own independence.

At times, the absence of wisdom in our children's choices may leave us stunned. A friend told me that when agonizing over her teenage daughter's waywardness, the Lord spoke to her and said, "Give your child the right to choose death if she wants to." That is really the heart of the Father toward the prodigal as we read in Luke chapter 15. When a daughter's college career is truncated due to an unwanted pregnancy, a son fathers a child out of wedlock, or an offspring drops out because of drugs or flunks due to depression, we can stay in rest, and reassure both our young person and ourselves that this crisis is not the screeching end of our hopes and dreams. It is the start of a new chapter that can be authored by God.

One mother I knew had two boys in prison but still displayed deep assurance in the rest, sovereignty, and sufficiency of her God. She and her husband always came to the monthly teachings that I held many years ago in a small English village. They took the same seats every time, faces upturned in worship and Bibles opened to receive from the Word of Truth. However bravely they appeared in public, though, their hearts were never stoical, only secure. Though the tears would flow, the mama would say, "We trust our God who is in control!" I saw them a few years ago still in the same sweet, trusting place, yet there was no evidence of change in their children's situation. God's good was evidenced in the Christlikeness of the parents' lives.

When I became pregnant, I was within months of graduating from nursing school. In those ancient days, no pregnant girl, whether married or not, was permitted to stay on and finish the course. It truly did seem like the end of my life, and I did consider ending it myself. I could not see then that I would marry the father of my baby and stay married for over forty years, to date. Thanks to a technicality (pre-ordained, I suspect!), I was able to sit my board exams and earn my nursing diploma. Our God is in the business of redemption and restoration. My sin brings me no shame when I see my beautiful, loving daughter, my son-in-love, her husband, and now their wonderful children, my three grandchildren. What an honor!

God Makes No Mistakes

When your children mess up, don't reach for the hair shirt

61

or beat yourself up for failing. Our children are free agents and will make choices of their own, quite independently of us. I know this is hard to understand when they are little and lie snuggled up in their sleepy beds in our tender care. Still, one day they will leave, and all may not always be well.

You may be familiar with the *nature—nurture—choice* paradigm. Although social scientists squabble over what degree of effect these three influences exert in our lives, it is generally believed that part of our child's personality is genetic, with certain proclivities passed on in the DNA; while their environment, the way we influence them, is only partly responsible for molding their character formation. Lastly, in my opinion, the largest determinant in their lives is their own freedom of choice.

No matter on which side you stand in these arguments, God is there as our children select and decide. He will be there when we cannot be and where we wouldn't want to be—at the all-night parties, the smoking of the first joint, the illicit tryst in the back seat of the car. I am only now learning about some of the capers my children got up to, and there are others that I'm sure I will never know. I am convinced that (to borrow a expression from the Queen of Sheba when she finally saw the much-lauded kingdom of King Solomon), "Not even the half has been told me."[5] This is not to be misconstrued as either condoning or resigning ourselves to our children's sinful capers. Only that, if they do succumb to temptation, our condemnation cannot change anything. Never forget that our gracious, unchanging God will use it for good in the long run.

Be glad and rejoice in His amazing ability to take care of our children. While we pray that God will keep them from evil, or at the very least take them out of the circumstances, to our horror He often permits our children to travel through the storms. Then, by the power of His indwelling life He delivers them safe, though scarred; secure, though shaken; and wiser, though wounded. And if, for any number of reasons they do not come through—or even when death snatches them from our aching breasts—then, more than ever, we must know that our God is good and just and in control.

The great German word *gestalt* has gained a place in our vocabulary. *Gestalt* sums up beautifully our goof-ups when God is in the equation. It implies a satisfying completion, a closed circle with no loose ends. It does not mean the end of a good thing, but that everything has worked out well. Whether in the momentous or the mundane, how great is the grace of our God.

Nourishing Nugget from *The Message:*

"Do you think anyone is going to be able to drive a wedge between us and Christ's love for us? There is no way! Not trouble, not hard times, not hatred, not hunger, not homelessness, not bullying threats, not backstabbing, not even the worst sins listed in Scripture" (Romans 8).

APPETIZERS

1 *Fully engage and enjoy the "little years,"
for they are so quickly over.*

2 *Before you know it, your calendar will be
clear, and both the telephone and the bathroom will be available all the time!*

3 *The empty nest is a misnomer. Children
bring home friends, spouses, and eventually,
more little ones.*

7

The Sound
of Silence

IN THE DEAFENING silence, I missed the shoes. Piles of sweaty sneakers heaped by the entryway or in the mudroom were a sure sign that all my children were home under my roof and my care. Whether they had returned for a short or long visit, when they left, the shoes went with them. The disappearance of the shoes, more than anything else, reminded me of my family's independence, their ability to simply walk away.

Not Little for Long

Long before they are able to walk, indeed from the moment we first hold our babies, we need to grasp the reality that their time with us is so short. This is hard to see when we are tackling mounds of dirty laundry in the morning after yet one more sleepless night. However, holding this fact foremost will not only let us more fully enter into the little years and enjoy our children with more patience, joy, and abandon; it will also prepare us for that inevitable day of their departure.

In the middle of all the noise, disorder, and a million interruptions during the years of raising our children, we will often long for silence. Following the crying, the squabbling, and the sibling rivalry, come the war zone sounds of computer games and the cacophonous sounds of the current pop music that even closed bedroom doors cannot contain. When my daughter's children were small, I asked her, "What do you want most for yourself?" Without a moment's hesitation, she quipped, "To be able to finish a sentence." Now when I pop by for a "cuppa" during the silence of the school day, we blissfully complete our every thought and sentence.

Danielle Crittenden describes the swift passing of the little years beautifully:

> The length of time it takes for a human being to transform from a demanding infant into a smiling baby into a crawling terror into a walking child into a teenager and finally into a grown man or woman is profoundly short. Years later, a mother looks at baby photos and hungrily tries to recall the powder scent of her children's skin, the soft indents on the back of their necks, the pudginess of their feet, how she could cradle their entire bodies in her arms. Where did that all go, so quickly?[1]

I suspect that mourning over our children leaving has as much to do with no longer feeling needed as it has to do with our adjusting to being alone. As I sat with a lonely mother in her living room, she had eyes for only one of the many family photographs hung around the room—the one in which her five children are huddled together smiling broadly for the camera with unselfconscious, innocent gaze when they were still all safe under her wing and clucking control. They were noisy and needy, and she was very necessary.

Sounds of Change

Mothers will either grieve or exult to varying degrees over

the departure of their children. The working mom may feel less guilty; the reluctant mother experiences relief that they are gone, and the stay-at-home mom may be eager to get out of the home herself. Regardless of the intensity of the experience, all of us will face the silence. This is the "empty nest." Someone has said that it is not empty until the family dog dies. Yes, I well remember that day of grief too. The difference is that we can, and do, easily fill our lives with more pets, while our children are not so easily replaced.

As mothers, this time of our lives can be one of the most excruciatingly painful places of change that we may ever endure. Give or take a few years, it usually lands on our doorstep about the same time as menopause marches in, or just as our own parents succumb to chronic or debilitating disease or death. Regrettably, divorce often occurs at this juncture—with the children gone, the only reason for many couples staying together is no longer there. The confluence of these events will certainly expose our readiness, or lack of it, for living life without children.

Even with the best preparation, we will still feel the loss. This is acceptable and healthy for it is indeed a loss, a change, and a challenge. I thought I was well prepared when it intersected with my rich, exciting, and fulfilling life directing and teaching in a women's ministry. After I returned home from zooming around the motorways and country lanes of Europe, I recall getting up in the middle of the night to steal away and weep. I remembered about "Rachel weeping for her children" (Jeremiah 31:15). In the bleak hours, the Holy Spirit comes in His role as Comforter reminding us that we have a continuing destiny and that weeping only endures for a night, "but joy comes in the morning" (Psalm 30:5).

It is also during this phase of our lives that we wake up next to the man who has lain beside us every night for many years, with whom we have savored coffee for many a morning, and now wonder who he is. When the children have gone, we may realize the need to re-acquaint ourselves with their father again. After so many years of raising children together, so many conversations revolving only around them—their shots, their schedules, their grades—we've forgotten how to talk about anything else. Whether we are partnered or not, we moms (and dads, too) are primarily responsible to and for ourselves before our God.

The first time I came face-to-face with the reality of life without children and life with only my husband was one summer when each of our children was spending some weeks away from home with friends and family in places as far apart as California and Scotland. Over the quiet breakfast table, I looked at the father of my children and was frightened at the prospect of a future with just him and me. Thankfully, it served as a wake-up call to start cultivating our friendship again, as well as attending to my own life.

For too many mothers the challenge at this point of life involves struggling to find out who we really are. Our entire life, it seems, has been devoted to our children. As I have already mentioned, we need to cultivate our own identity throughout our mothering years so we are ready for the silence that follows their leaving. However, even if we have not done so, it is never too late to start. The worst insult to add at this injurious interlude would be to wallow in self-pity, paralysis, or fear of the future. There are years left to go, and opportunities abound to join organizations, volunteer, return to school, or travel.

Increasing, Not Decreasing

Whatever determinations, desires, or dreams we still want

to fulfill, the first place to look is within. Don't look for direction from the Web or from resources at the local library. Jesus told the woman at the well that He would give water as a "well of life springing up from the inside that would never run dry" (John 4:13,14). That is our starting point. In what direction is the water of your soul flowing?

At a Mother's Day tea held at my grandson's kindergarten class this spring (where grandmothers were welcome too) I saw another grandmother look wistfully over the clamoring classroom and comment, "I wish I was back in these days. It sure beats watching TV." Her outlook saddened me; but that is the danger we risk if we have never cultivated a life outside of mothering. Jacqueline Kennedy Onassis said:

> What is sad for women of my generation is that they weren't supposed to work if they had families. What were they to do when the children were grown—watch the raindrops coming down the windowpane?[2]

Silence will descend for all of us at some stage, and as we gaze out the window, the only drops falling may be our own tears. But, cheer up! Your calendar is clear, both the telephone and the bathroom are available all the time, and now it is time to reclaim your own life.

We will continue to be mothers even when they are gone and our counsel will still be solicited—albeit selectively! This is the day for which we raised them; so we do not want our sorrow to eclipse their joy. The best send-off we can ever give our growing and going children is to wave them goodbye with the merry, full heart of a mother now about to become her own woman again. We must be as independent of them as they are of us.

A young mother once told me that she lost the first few

years of her marriage because her mother would not release her. The need to hold on extended to the place where she actually faked terminal illness to keep her daughter's attention. The daughter was duped, and it destroyed the foundational years of her nascent marriage. It is good to note here the necessity of leaving and cleaving on the married child's part.

And guess what? Like all of Satan's ploys to steal, kill, and destroy, the empty nest is a lie. My sage daughter first pointed out the fallacy of this statement when I was whining over the silence and solitude at home. As I glanced over at the family group photo taken one Christmas when we all gathered from our various venues around the country, I concluded she was right. There I saw that, beside my original three children, there were now three spouses and six of their children, my grandchildren. The sound of silence was shattered with more noise than I could sometimes manage to handle during family events. I had not diminished, but increased.

The settling silence can rise and resound with the praise and joy of a contented heart. Yours. And mine. The anticipation of all that awaits us in Christ is like a thundering applause for His faithfulness as He continues to fulfill in us that to which we were called from before the foundation of the world. It is time now to pick up our own shoes from the hallway and get going.

Nourishing Nuggets from *The Message:*

"Jesus said, 'Anyone who drinks the water I give will never thirst—not ever. The water I give will be an artesian spring within, gushing fountains of endless life'" (John 4).

"Yahweh, my Shepherd! I don't need a thing. You have bedded me down in lush meadows, You find me quiet pools from which to drink. True to Your Word, You let me catch my breath and send me in the right direction" (Psalm 23).

APPETIZERS

1 *Sometimes grandmothers interfere in an attempt to make up for their own flawed mothering.*

2 *Grandparents can be carriers of lifegiving "oxygen."*

8

The
No Meddling Zone

"YOU CAN'T LEAVE me, Mom," I whimpered. "I don't know what to do." As I nuzzled my new baby who was but a week old, I panicked at the prospect of my mother leaving me alone with her first-born grandchild. My mother, nicknamed "the sage," lived up to her reputation and wisely replied, "You will find your own methods and means without me." She set the stage for modeling, not meddling, and I suspect she already knew well that neither mothers nor grandmothers could be everywhere, but God is. This chapter is written from the grandmother's perspective, yet will be enlightening to her daughter for it will give valuable insight into the mother she may find puzzling or even troubling at times.

Setting Healthy Boundaries
Since that moment with my first baby, I have become a grandmother many times over. I'm not sure I have always done as well as my own mother in letting go. I have had to spend some extended time with some of my grandchildren while their mamas continued to work for a while, and that has not only bonded me to them, but also made me feel more responsible for their welfare. I have struggled with boundary issues; but I am thankful that I have grown children who are able to let me

know when I am trespassing into their territory, and that I have a tender enough heart to hear both them and the Lord.

Defining roles and setting boundaries are essential elements in all healthy relationships and imperative between grandmother and mother if the flow of family interaction is to be smooth, sustaining, and satisfying. One of the chief criticisms I hear from mothers is that grandmothers are liable to interfere when they disapprove of the way she is raising her children. Grandmothers may misguidedly feel obligated to redress the balance of their own mothering. A popular quip says: to grandparents, grandchildren can do no wrong, while their parents can do no right!

Although we hear more and more of grandparents' rights being both challenged and claimed in court, learning early to relinquish our grip on our own offspring sets the stage for healthy, happy, and helpful relationships with our grandchildren, too. Conflicts are minimal for the grandmother and mother who have learned, or are continuing to learn that neither can be all-in-all for their children and that God is the true Parent. Mutual recognition of heavenly parentage will assure harmony, respect, and love that reflect the Father's heart for earthly families.

It is well recognized that even when we are adults, parents still have a huge influence on our lives. One of the deepest ways that a grandmother can impact her daughter, the mother, is by reminding her that in Christ she has all the wisdom, love, and grace that she will ever need to be a parent. Then, we need to back off and prove we mean it by not meddling! In yet another reference to the book of Job (a character I believe is a composite of everyman), the young counselor Elihu, having let the elders speak first could wait no longer to state his opinion once he'd seen that being older did not render the other counselors wiser. He declared that the spirit of God gives wisdom that has nothing to do with age.[1] Giving the young mother that kind of encouragement is enabling and empowering and creates an atmosphere conducive to her asking for advice and counsel from the rich repository of the grandmother's experience.

Life-Giving Oxygen

A grandmother's influence is enormous and the love she has for her grandchildren defies description. As much as I thought I adored my own children, when the next generation came along, love ambushed me. However, we do not have the responsibility for their care in the way we did as a mother. With feelings so intense, a dichotomy emerges right from the outset. Nonetheless, although we are not the primary caregivers, our input can be important and effective. Madeleine L'Engle, who is through her books one of my favorite mentors, writes:

> What a teacher or librarian or parent can do, in working with children, is to give the flame enough oxygen so that it can burn. As far as I am concerned, this providing of oxygen is one of the noblest of all vocations.[2]

My maternal grandmother fanned a flame in my young life, subsequently sparking a fire that spread the length and breadth of my homeland of Great Britain. She whispered to me, in what I describe as a frozen frame in time, the precise context of which I have long since forgotten, "You cannot love anyone else until you love yourself." That cardinal truth became the life-giving oxygen that fired my heart and lit the torches of hope, faith, and power many years later when I led a women's ministry.

The ripple effects of the influence we have on our grandchildren will extend beyond our lifetime. Whatever we sow into their lives, let's be sure that it is life-giving. When my first grandchild, Caleb, was very small we used to play card games such as Uno. I have never been able to shuffle cards with the adroitness that everyone else seems to possess. The way folks cut and flick the pack is beyond my capabilities. My dear grandson's consoling comment was, "You may not be good at shuffling cards, Nana, but you know how to tell your grandchildren about Jesus."

Even if relationships were not good with one's own children, the arrival of the next generation offers tremendous possibilities for repair and enrichment, for these little ones come with their receptors ready to receive all the devotion that we are so ready to transmit. Simply living in honesty and integrity has a profound impact on their young lives, although we may be unconscious of the transforming power we exert when walking uprightly. I like what Nancy Parker Brummett writes:

> We can have the feeling of being at home in many locations …It's also a blessing we protect by keeping our opinions about houses, decorating, and child-rearing to ourselves—unless they ask, of course![3]

While we may not be able to reform the changing mores that affect the family today, we can walk in compassion, wisdom, and discretion, doing our best to accommodate the changes without being censorious. Many more mothers work outside the home today, which produces different patterns of parenting. Divorce is, sadly, now almost as frequent in families of faith as in those without that foundation. In those cases, grandmothers may find themselves assisting in the care of the children—and, in some cases, actually raising them.

Pray More, Say Less

What our adult children always need from their mothers is unconditional love, support, and approval of their efforts in difficult circumstances. "Pray more and say less" might be a fitting little maxim by which to live in these relationships. They do not need difficult parents at any point in their lives. No matter how we might feel about the spouse, who is the father or mother of our precious grandchild, interfering will only end up alienating us from one another. Remember, the grandchild will always be loyal to his or her parent, and we will lose out all around by criticizing or meddling. Except in cases of grave abuse and neglect where we are obligated both by law and love to intervene, our best stance is support sans censorship, but with prayer.

When I am tempted to quibble and complain concerning certain behaviors in my grown family, the Holy Spirit never fails to remind me of my own weaknesses that others would have observed with equal disapproval when I was raising my children. Moreover, when I do yield to temptation and shoot a sharp rebuke, I have the opportunity to model penitence and ask forgiveness, further fortifying my humanity and reliance on my heavenly Parent. Each one of us makes her own mistakes and thereby learns dependence on God alone.

I love what Carolyn G. Heilbrun writes in *The Last Gift of Time*. "All children will eventually consider themselves able to be better parents than their parents were. And so they should."[4] Our children may well consider us far better grandparents than we were parents. A good friend's daughter said of her father in his role as grandpa to her little boy, "He is not the same man that I remember as my dad."

A Legacy of Love

For what do we want to be remembered? What is the

legacy we want to leave behind? Finding and maintaining balance in our interactions with our adult children, their spouses, and their children will supply us, in the remaining years of our lives, a role as diverse and demanding as it was to raise our own children. Then, as now, we conclude that we cannot oversee and manage everyone's life, no matter how much wisdom and insight we have accrued over the years. Still the banner is, I cannot be everywhere, but the God of all generations is. When God births us into His family through Christ, that connection, that union, gives us access to a kind of love that overlooks every failure and shortcoming, that covers a multitude of mistakes.[5]

Families are ideally suited for such an experiment because errors and misunderstandings abound on every side. Children will fault parents for any number of things, from interfering to ignoring. Grandparents will arrive at erroneous conclusions about their grown children's motives and methods. As water is the universal solvent in the physical realm, love is the all-purpose dissolver of differences, large and small in the spiritual and soul realm. The currency of love we leave behind will be what they make withdrawals on to resolve their own issues and solve their own problems. Then, confident in the love that flows both ways, we can safely and assuredly leave our grown children to be their own kind of parent, finding their own methods and means in the freedom that allows God to be God in their lives.

Nourishing Nuggets from *The Message:*

"So tend to your knitting. You've got your hands full just taking care of your own life before God. Forget about deciding what's right for each other. Here's what you need to be concerned about: that you don't get in the way of someone else, making life more difficult than it already is" (Romans 14).

"Most of all, love each other as if your life depended on it. Love makes up for practically anything" (1 Peter 4).

APPETIZERS

❶ *Your children's dad may be struggling with his own role as a man, husband, and father.*

❷ *Mothers bonding too closely with their children may marginalize the children's father.*

❸ *Many dads are aching to be more involved, intimate, and engaged with their children.*

9

Dealing With Dads

MY FRIEND'S WARM brown eyes filled with tears that spilled unrelentingly down her pretty face. Over coffee and cookies, she spoke of her baby son's death as if it were a week ago. "My ex-husband blamed me for the genetic disorder that our baby inherited from my side of the family." The pain was as fresh as the smell from the nearby bakery although the bereavement occurred a decade earlier.

Balancing Father and Child

This is a book for mothers. It is specifically designed to include those who may not have the father of their child living with them like the mother quoted above, or in homes where the father may not even be in the picture. I want such mothers to identify with all the aspects that we have discussed, without feeling marginalized or manipulated into guilt due to their solo status. However, by definition, one cannot be a mother without a father featuring somewhere in the equation. We are inexorably bound together with the fathers of our children. It is not in the scope of this book to deal with partnership, marriage, or even the father as he relates, or does not relate, to his children. This chapter is concerned with how we mothers deal with fathers, how their presence—or lack of it—affects our lives.

Before we consider the father's influence, we do well to first look at ourselves. In what behaviors are we engaging that may require alteration for us to live in harmony with the father of our children? I have learned much in the course of preparing this book, especially through the many interviews I have conducted. One mother to five natural, one adopted, and several foster children left me with a profound thought. She said, "We are one flesh with our husband, not with our child." From the beginning, we set out to raise our children to leave and cleave. When mothers attach unwholesomely to their offspring, fathers are marginalized and left out of the equation. My mother gave me wise advice when my first baby was born: "Love your baby, but do not forget your husband." Unfortunately, as my husband is acutely aware, I did not always follow this advice!

We need to attend to the balance between our children and their father. Sometimes we marginalize him because we are overprotective and can, in certain cases, be inordinately bonded to our children, particularly the first-born son. This nexus has deep roots in history, culture, and religion. In ancient Athenian culture, the husband could tell his wife that if their child was a girl it was to be cast out; but if a boy, to let it live. This is still true in some societies today; and, even in as innocuous a setting as the delightful musical *Oklahoma* (which I saw for the umpteenth time recently), the preference for a male child surfaces. Because this chapter was on my front burner at the time I saw the musical, I found myself hearing the words of Curly with a fresh perspective. In the course of his wooing Laurey, he eagerly anticipates their future, which he hopes will include a couple of boys!

However, the very sons that a father so covets can become a threat to his relationship with the mother of that child. A mother feels so proud and successful when she produces a child that brings such honor, yet the father may end up feeling neglected in the exchange. It fact, it is highly possible for a mother to love her children, whether boys or girls, more than the father of her children. Because children consume our energies, we may see in their arrival a source of satisfaction and fulfillment that is missing in our marriage.

Untenable Expectations

Fathering has now taken on a more prominent profile, approaching almost cult status, both nationally and internationally. There is now a proliferation of supportive organizations as men around the world are awakening to the call to be fathers who are more involved with their children. I counted ten such organizations in my state alone. Much of the impetus for this stems from concern for fathers' rights—rights for divorced fathers where custody normally goes to the mother, and the abortion issue, where the fathers' rights are rarely considered.

Parenting was designed to be a joint endeavor that provides the exquisite male/female balance and beauty of our great God's design for the family. When such is not the case, mending this rift requires both genders to be aware of the divide and participate in the healing. In order to build a bridge to close this gap we must first demolish the existing designations that separate men and women. By denying women the right to fulfill their cultural call outside the confines of the home with dignity and without guilt, we keep the divide and the disparity alive. And when we exclude men from the process of child rearing, they are diminished and denied the kind of intimacy with their progeny that their heavenly Father intended.

Of course, for many reasons, there are fathers who do not want that kind of intimacy. One day while writing this book, I went for a massage. Before I ever got onto the table to enjoy my longed-for luxury, I spent an hour listening to my massage therapist who, once she knew the title of this book, spontaneously shared the ache, the agony, the legalities of dealing with the dad of her little boy. I listened to her relate the pain she had endured as she wiped the tears away from her hurt, bewildered little boy when dad failed, yet again, to show up for the Little League game. And the distress of dealing with her own conflicting emotions as wife and mother in the middle, and the lack of money from a deadbeat dad.

Delinquent fathers are legion. During time spent with another single mom whose husband had abandoned her with their two tiny two-year-olds, I wondered aloud how men could desert their children, never mind their wives. "I wish you could ask him that question," was her reply. I would surely follow this lead were I to write a book on this topic.

The weight of the hierarchical imprint is heavy, and the burden it places on a father is often underestimated. This is perhaps never better exemplified than in the threat mothers often level at their misbehaving youngsters: "Just wait until your father gets home!" The father of my own children recently told me how much he hated and recoiled from this role—a task that put him in a harsher, more authoritarian light than that of the mother who is perfectly capable of executing the appropriate and immediate discipline herself. An insightful husband and wife team has written:

> An approach to marriage that calls for rigid hierarchy ignores the variety of gifts and personality types God has built into both women and men.[1]

Under the untenable expectation of being the sole head of the household, having the final say, and keeping it all together, fathers falter, collapse, and sometimes flee. If not literally, often figuratively, and frequently emotionally, even while they remain in the home. Paul R. Smith puts this most poignantly:

> We live in an age of the absent father. The Industrial Revolution has taken fathers out of the home, away from their wives and children, and placed them in inaccessible factories and offices. They are missing physically and psychologically. Men no longer spend long hours alongside their daughters and sons in the family business or on the family farm. Today many of us live with a great father wounding, especially those of us who are sons. We long for our missing fathers, someone to initiate us into the world of manhood and breathe into us an understanding of what it means to be a man. The male soul has been left shriveled and unaffirmed for want of good fathering.[2]

A Father's Heart

Therein lies another reason why mothers overcompensate. We assume a dual role, both our own and the one that the daddy declines or is unable to do. Tragically and unconscionably, religion too often perpetuates the hierarchy that separates men and women and insists on the father taking a unilateral, authoritative role, simply because of his gender. The Greek word *kephalē,* which is translated "head" in the Pauline Epistles, connotes "source, nurturing life, or completion," not "ruler or boss" as it is commonly translated in English and cripplingly applied to the marriage relationship.[3] This is a hard and constricting role for many mothers. Until the father finds this liberty, mothers will have to lean on the life within to co-create a home where love rules overall.

This love compensates for children with imbalanced

parenting, mothers who are frustrated and unfulfilled, and fathers who flounder in a role for which they are, by design, inadequate to fulfill on their own.

Ruth Haley Barton writes:

After listening to some of the women's frustrations about being overlooked and stereotyped at work, one man shared, 'Really the whole thing about work stinks. I would really like to be home with my kids. I try to work out of the home as much as I can, and right now my wife and I are trying to figure out how we can be more of a team in our marriage and in our parenting.'[4]

Whether we find ourselves coupled or solo (especially if daddy is absent because he is deceased), it behooves us to trust the fatherhood of God instead of our own ubiquitous motherhood. There is no need to singularly assume entire responsibility for our children's welfare—body, soul, and spirit. Mothers have often been duped into this god-like stance. Then we fail to observe the common enemy of our souls skulking away undetected, while we view our spouse as the adversary.

If there is one lesson we need to learn in painful relationships, it is that we are not engaging in battle with our fellow human beings. Your spouse is not the enemy; Satan is the sower of discord and strife that engages us in battle with each other. While we hurl accusations, evade responsibility, and become bitterly entrenched, our children suffer; and we are all diminished.

Love for our children will demand that we honor, encourage, and respect their fathers as much as possible. When we feel we are flying solo, the co-pilot missing and unsupportive, we need to let our heavenly Parent take competent charge of the controls and bring us in for a safe and sane landing. Even in the most acrimonious of situations, we never want to poison our children toward their dad. That same love we have toward our children will be as adamant in guarding our own hearts so that no one can emotionally hold us ransom for the past, present, or future. Remember, love never fails.

If we remember that many fathers are aching for more involvement with their precious progeny, it will keep us tender towards the daddy of our children. We are not the only ones dealing with frustration and stereotypes. Hear the words of a dear friend and devoted, divorced dad:

> In terms of our parenting abilities, I moved beyond all the false noise of the world. The posturing for superiority between men and women truly disgusted me. The simple truth is that God made us to parent together. Each has unique strengths and challenges as a parent. My calling is to do what is right by my son. Both of us allowed the spirit of God's grace to soften the edges of all this and transform the pain into kindness.

The result is a triumph for the child whose father is still willing to be a vital part of his or her life despite the battle of a broken home.

It is cause for great celebration when we find a home where the dad is totally present and involved with his little ones, champions his wife in her role as woman and mother, and knows his own place as a partner in the parenting program. I am honored to know a father who does just that. He calls himself, "Dad at Home." He speaks movingly of his two children for whom he has assumed the daily care, while his wife, their mom, pursues her career. Hear his wonderful words as he describes moments of interaction with his children:

I am overwhelmed with a sense of pride. My daughter comes to dad for answers to her queries with a trust and vulnerability that takes my breath away. I've seen my son's happiness on too many occasions to be able to count them, his eyes shining with a love that would melt a glacier.

Though such intimate involvement is somewhat rare, and it is increasingly common that mothers are confronting absent and uncaring fathers, we are still never hampered from pursuing our destiny. She whom Christ has made free is free indeed. God has promised to be Father to the fatherless, thereby releasing mothers from the burden of dual parenting. Whether the tears we shed are from the wounds of today, the pain of the distant past, or fear of the future, with Abba on our side, we are dealing with a Dad who will never desert us, abandon us, or blame us.

Nourishing Nuggets from *The Message:*

"Father of orphans, champion of widows, is God in His holy house" (Psalm 68).

"This resurrection life you received from God is not a timid, grave-tending life. It's adventurously expectant, greeting God with a childlike 'What's next, Papa?' God's Spirit touches our spirits and confirms who we really are. We know who He is, and we know who we are: Father and children. And we know we are going to get what's coming to us—an unbelievable inheritance!" (Romans 8).

🌹 APPETIZERS

1 *Failure to forgive yourself and efforts to pay the penalty for your own failures result in false guilt, resentment, and disease.*

2 *Forgiveness is forever flowing from the heart of God—an unplumbed river of grace always available for every infraction.*

10

Shedding the Skin of Guilt

WHEN A MAN was asked why he was rolling around in cactus in the desert, he replied, "It seemed like a good idea at the time." Dr. William Glasser, one of my mental health mentors, used that anecdote frequently in his lectures. It gives insight into the genesis of guilt. Many of the things we do as mothers, for which we later chide ourselves, in fact seemed like good ideas at the time.

Real and Imagined Guilt

It is both liberating and comforting to remember that most of what we do that causes us guilt, is done out of ignorance, immaturity, or weakness. The most common guilt generators among mothers seem to be anger and impatience. One perfectionist mom driven to raise her two boys to mythical standards, told me that she was always worried about not getting it right. When pressed for an explanation of what "right" was, she did not know, nor was anybody able to tell her. A couple of Thanksgivings ago, I wondered whether it was right, due to time constraints, to resort to instant potatoes instead of the traditional homemade variety. I opened the package, added water, and no one even noticed the difference. All those years of peeling potatoes and trying to impress!

Whether you are suffering guilt in a current situation or looking back with regret over paths not taken, the intent of this chapter is to bring hope, relief, and peace. We torture ourselves with suffocating, searing soliloquies for our mistakes in child raising:

"How could I...?"
"Why didn't I...?"
"I wish..."
"If only..."

Our self-condemnations wrap themselves around us so tightly that we are unable to either inhale or exhale forgiveness. We are professional travel agents for guilt trips, and in our minds we journey many miles to multiple destinations of self denigration.

The cartoonist Cathy Guiswaite even included mothers in the four major guilt groups, along with love, food, and career. While we age, we are constantly shedding our natural skin, while new cells continue to replace them. It would appear that, in the emotional realm, we do not shed, but actually accrue more layers as the years go by. It is time to shed the grimy skin of guilt.

The dictionary defines guilt as:

a) the state of one who has committed an offense, esp. consciously; b) feelings of culpability, esp. for imagined offenses or from a sense of inadequacy; self-reproach.[1]

So guilt can be either factual or manufactured. The guilt that we fabricate, that our imaginations fertilize over the years, can grow into a monster. The source of this guilt is not hard to find. Remember, we have believed that God could not be every-where, so He made mothers. We think that we can control cir-cumstances; when we fail to live up to that lofty call, we grasp for guilt in order to pay the penalty for our failure to be god-like. We accept blame too readily for we are, after all, supposed to be in charge and should have done better. Imagined guilt is a ruthless enemy of our souls. Satan is our accuser, and when we listen to that voice, the same voice that promised godhood to the human race a long time ago, it continues to convince us of our divinity as we clutch at our fig leaf of pride, crouching in fear, hiding from the heart of God.

Sweet Fragrance of Forgiveness

For both the perceived guilt (that sprouts out of pride) and the actual infractions that we have committed, forgiveness is the only antidote. Genuine guilt is a gift, for through it we have the opportunity to change. If we fail to feel guilt for real violations, somewhere along the way we have lost our tenderness and trac-tability, probably due to hurt and disillusionment. Forgiveness is forever flowing and cleanses us immediately upon confession.[2] As we shared in an earlier chapter, just as the little child is quick to grant us absolution, so too is God. The trouble lies in forgiv-ing ourselves. Our reluctance to forgive ourselves springs from our thinking that we should sometime, somehow, reach a state of not failing.

A prominent Chinese Christian's experience illustrates this well. He was in the habit of confessing his sins at the close of each day. Finally, he grew disgusted with the repeti-tion of his failures and cried out to his Lord that surely such a great Christian should perform more perfectly! The reply he received that day set him free from his efforts to attain perfection. He heard his heavenly Parent say that He did not expect anything else of him but to make mistakes.

Psychiatrist Dr. Glasser used guilt as a verb, which helps us to see our personal responsibility for choosing "to guilt, or not to guilt."[3] "Guilting" simply creates another mistake, this time against ourselves. Jesus said that whatever we have done unto the least, we have done unto Him.[4] Even if we consider ourselves in the "least" category, we are still eligible to receive the gift of forgiveness, and when we fail to receive that remission, we slight the Jesus in us. The means of absolving guilt is at hand. We do not share the plight of the gentlewoman in Shakespeare's Macbeth. She moaned over the blood on the hands of the one who had planned the murder of the king. "All the perfumes of Arabia will not sweeten this little hand," she cried. But the sweet perfume of forgiveness stands in stark contrast to the gall of guilt. Jesus Christ provided for our absolution and freedom from guilt through the sweet-smelling sacrifice of His death. Unresolved or repressed guilt results in bitter, resentful mothers. A physician has said,

> Resentment is a toxic emotion. Not anger, (but) resentment. You can turn anger into a healing modality because it is a highly charged passion. If you turn anger on yourself, it turns into depression. If you turn anger against yourself and hold on to it, you start resenting life, your boss, your spouse. This is a negative, powerful emotion, and it can cause disease.[5]

However, bitterness is never more powerful than God's love to cleanse the toxins of guilt. I met up with a long-time friend recently and, as is wont of people with "some chronology," we ended up exchanging tales of the toll that time takes on our bodies. We both agreed that the pain of arthritis flares as a warning of stress, such as when we assume the role of a mother who thinks she has to be everywhere and solve everything, from the care of aging parents to the divorce of a grown child. If you are not so advanced in decades at the time of reading this, take heart—you may be able to avoid many diseases by the simple expedient of letting go and letting God.

Redemption and Release

There is another kind of guilt—guilt that, until we become aware of it, we cannot cast off. I refer to the kind of culpability that we must acknowledge before repentance and restitution can result. When our adult children in crises unearth pathology from childhood that affects their functioning, we mothers become cognizant of our unwitting contribution to the equation, and guilt is the first freezing emotion. In my case, this guilt miraculously thawed under the warm love of my grown child who was willing to forgive my ignorance; what could have become an unyielding iceberg of bitterness became a horizonless ocean of freedom for both mother and child. Even in the regrettable circumstance where forgiveness from the offended adult child is not forthcoming, we must rest assured that we stand exonerated in God's eyes.

Our God is in the business of redemption. There is no need to wear a hair shirt to constantly remind ourselves of our culpability, as certain monks would do in order to keep themselves ever-mindful of their sin. Our heavenly Parent wants to restore and turn to good every past deed we deplore and everything for which we are ashamed, the memories from which we recoil.

I glean comfort from the encounter that Jesus had with Peter following the resurrection. He met this renegade disciple on the beach after his night of fruitless fishing, a task Peter had eschewed to follow his Lord. Just a few days earlier, Peter had vehemently denied, disparaged and deserted his Master when He needed His disciples most, at the crucifixion. However, instead of a diatribe, Jesus delivered breakfast and deluged the impetuous Peter with love—a love and forgiveness that eradicated all of Peter's guilt.[6]

The more we depend on that resurrection life that is in us, the more readily we will substitute forgiveness for guilt. Our shedding of guilt is in direct proportion to our trust and confidence in God's utter, unconditional approval of us, no matter what. The measure of mercy we have for ourselves will dictate how merciful and forgiving we are toward our children. And they will grieve and disappoint us many times over, whether they paint the walls with permanent markers, stay out past curfew, or drop out of college. The strong God-love that is in us will forgive them over and over again.

Times and temperatures change in our relationships with our children. There are those sunny and bright days when we all bask in the warmth of family at its finest. And then there are the dark and gloomy days where the clouds come barreling in and we shiver in the cold of alienation and fear. These are the rhythms of life. We are never expected to be everywhere, do everything right, or be entirely responsible for our children's choices; so there is no need to chafe forever under the relentless ribbing of regret. Still, since starting this book, I have had a recurring dream of going back to live in the house where I raised my children, somehow wanting to return and change the way I did things. But, there is no way back.

Nevertheless, we can be free. Being relieved of our guilt does not mean we deny or forget what we did, but we no longer hold it to our own account. We can choose to be co-creators with our Lord in working it for good as we walk in the liberty of His limitless love, and encourage other mothers to believe that nothing is beyond His ability or willingness to forgive.

So, let's get up out of the cactus patch where we have been trying to shed our grimy skin of guilt, and run to the lush, long-grassed, soothing meadow of God's glorious grace where the river that runs through it is called forgiveness.

Nourishing Nuggets from *The Message:*

"Think of it! All sins forgiven, the slate wiped clean, that old arrest warrant canceled and nailed to Christ's cross. He stripped all the spiritual tyrants in the universe of their sham authority at the cross and marched them naked through the streets" (Colossians 2).

"'I'll forever wipe the slate clean of their sins.' Once sins are taken care of for good, there's no longer any need to offer sacrifices for them" (Hebrews 10).

*A*PPETIZERS

1 *Jesus is your conquering hero. He shattered every stereotype of women during His earthly life.*

2 *In His death, He bought your freedom; and in His resurrection, He imbued you with His very own life.*

3 *When you choose intimacy with Christ over intimidation by the crowd, you will run forever free.*

11

Shattering
the Stereotypes

MY FINGERS were small and not very strong, but I wanted to peel potatoes with my mother. I can still smell the pungent, loamy earth that covered the big bucket-full of homegrown tubers. At the same time, I can still hear her firm yet gentle voice say, "My little one, your hands were meant for better things than peeling potatoes."

I felt slighted at the time, and I still consider peeling potatoes a noble and necessary chore as I demonstrated right up until that Thanksgiving when I decided to use the instant variety! But, the seed my mother sowed into my life that day has produced a harvest that took me beyond domesticity.

Just as my father imprinted on me that my gender was no hindrance to achievement, so my mom encouraged me to break the stereotype for women of her generation. My parents were people of the earth and sea; small farmers and fishermen in the Shetland Islands of Scotland. With such emancipated-thinking parents, how could I be anything but a champion of women and an advocate for a liberating look at motherhood?

Our Conquering Hero

The first and greatest liberator of women was none other than Jesus Christ. The world into which He was born was distinctly divided into male and female spheres of service. He came into an ancient world where, only 300 years earlier, the Greek philosopher Aristotle had deemed that women lacked the natural capacity for virtue. He came into a world where it was believed that women merely provided the soil into which man planted his seed. Sadly, this view still stubbornly sticks in some circles.

We are quite unconsciously immersed in the values, beliefs, and practices that shape the age in which we live. It is crucial to consider the existing culture and understand the scriptures in an accurate historical context. Then, when we read the accounts of Jesus' interactions with the female gender, we can clearly appreciate how revolutionary He really was. As one of many examples, look at the woman with the issue of blood.[1] In defiance of all the Levitical laws, she touched Jesus and, even more amazingly, He did not conform to the custom of the day by then declaring Himself unclean.[2] And she called out to Him in a culture that declared it shameful to hear a woman's voice in public.

Then there was the woman who had had an infirmity for eighteen years and whom Jesus healed on the Sabbath. She would have come from the segregated section of the synagogue, from the women's gallery. Yet He noticed her, and called her to come to Him. Consider also the prostitute who washed His feet.[3] The crown jewel of them all was the Samaritan woman at the well. The latter belonged to an ethnic group with whom no Jew associated, and she had had multiple partners. It was from this humble hand that the Creator of the universe took a drink to slake His thirst. He in turn gave her the life-giving water that would satisfy her soul. To this woman He entrusted the life-changing message of redemption that she joyfully declared throughout the entire town.[4]

Patriarchy Presides

My heart swells with gratitude and immeasurable love when I recount the stories that flesh out the heart of God in His Son. Long before He went to His sacrificial death, He was about His Father's business: the business of loving, liberating, and equalizing. He was intent on shattering the stereotypical strongholds of His day, especially as they related to the underdog. Women certainly qualified for that category. A Jewish man's morning mantra was, according to the Talmud, "Blessed are you, Lord our God, ruler of the universe, who has not created me a woman."

What happened to Jesus' magnificent modeling of emancipation? What happened to the leveling of the ground at the Cross where every divide, distance, and demerit was eradicated? Two thousand years later, we are still searching for the consummation of that liberation among the shards of enlightenment glistening in the dust of the centuries. The early church fathers and great devotional dons of the church held, scarcely without exception, an unemancipated view of women. Although we are indebted to them for so much that has enriched our Christian lives, we need to honestly acknowledge some of the statements attributed to these ancients regarding women and the ongoing influence their beliefs have had, particularly in the church. To name only a few: Thomas Aquinas considered woman defective and misbegotten. Augustine blamed the Flood on women. The Reformation brought scant relief for the female gender when Luther, blaming Eve as the mother of sin, said he could hardly speak of her without shame.

The Feminine Characteristics of God

I believe that much of the shame, second-class status, and stereotyping that women endure is due to the entrenched patriarchy still in place, the product of an exclusively paternal picture of God. God is no more male than female. He is Spirit. Apart from the male form that Jesus put on while He was in the flesh, the descriptors we have of God may be considered metaphors. The Scriptures ascribe to Him the qualities of a rock, a fortress, a lion; yet He is obviously not literally any of these things.[5] However, we feel the security of a rock, the safety of a fortress and the strength of a lion in our God. Why then, if He is genderless, is it important to be aware of His feminine attributes? Because we think in pictures. With female metaphors we can see the feminine characteristics of God—but not a goddess! The male/female nature of the eternal, living Deity has nothing to do with the pantheistic or polytheistic gods and goddesses of other religions. The Lord our God is one God.

There are multitudes of female metaphors in the Scriptures. In the Old Testament, God says He will cry out like a woman in labor, will gasp and pant.[6] How wondrously we, as mothers, can relate here. To think that God chooses to identify with us in such a moment of great pain and apprehension is awesome and comforting beyond any epidural anesthesia. In another part of the book of Isaiah, the prophet paints a vivid word picture of birthing, nursing, and consoling. Although the biblical text is describing the birth of the nation of Israel, the words are those with which we, as mothers, immediately identify. God says of His role in this process that He will comfort the newborn nation as a mother comforts her child.[7]

These are all glorious images to which we readily relate as we snuggle our baby at the breast, squeeze our toddler in the safety of our embrace, and "kiss it better" as we hold our hurting little one on our lap.

Then, how could we miss the telling female metaphor that describes our very entrance into the Kingdom of God? Jesus says that we must be born again. Peter in his letters uses a graphic metaphor that paints a picture of parentage from imperishable seed with divine heredity.[8] The medieval Christian mystic Meister Eckhart posed a probing question to which he readily supplied the answer, "What does God do all day long? God gives birth. From all eternity God lies on a maternity bed giving birth."

We need the feminine characteristics of God. The high profile that Mary the mother of Jesus holds in some religious circles attests to the need people feel for this facet of God. But, as highly lauded as Mary is as a mother, and as venerated as she is in Christian heritage, such prominence seems to have done little to enhance mothering in general. For that we should be grateful, for it serves to show God's intent from the beginning— His plan to complete everything and every person in Christ alone. Mothers are no exception. An insightful, anonymous contributor to the readers' letters in *Union Life* magazine writes,

> In Christ all that is feminine interacts in harmony with all that is masculine. His is the spirit of wholeness, of receptivity to God's sovereign will in union with the creative expression of that will. For me it is therapeutic to realize that I have been born again into a new family, the family of God in whom old dysfunctional patterns of male-female conflicts do not exist.

Indeed our God knows how to be both mother and father. Perhaps the greatest title for God, and that which comes closest to who He is no matter the exegesis, the era, or the eventuality is *I AM*. That designation fills every unmet need, answers every cry for identity, and mollifies every marginalized group in society. It is how God described Himself to Moses when that leader wondered how he would defend his assignment. "I AM has sent me to you."[9] Jesus assigned the same designation to

Himself when interacting with the religious leaders of His day.[10] Our Parent God is ever present, available, and all-encompassing in His tender, tenacious care.

Our Franchise from Heaven

What has been present from the beginning is the imprint of God's pervasive, exquisite egalitarianism. We see it in the creation when He made us in His image, male and female, showing His own wholeness. We see it in the far reaches of antiquity when the daughters of Job were given an inheritance along with their brothers, an action unheard of at that time.[11] And we know its culmination in the oneness and unity we, as women of a new creation, enjoy. Unlike women in much of the Muslim world, who are still veiled and silenced, we can both see and speak clearly; the veil of ignorance, imposition, and restriction has been removed in Christ. As we emerge emancipated out of obscurity, we have a great light to shine into the darkness in which women of every group still grope and fall. As we stumble out of the shadows of ignorance and imposition, our paths will flood with heaven's light and our lungs fill with the pristine air of freedom that flows from God, our heavenly Parent.

When we walk as free women, we also walk as strong, effective, and confident mothers. The imperative of learning Christ as our life, depending wholeheartedly on God as our source, and reveling in the unconditional love of our heavenly Parent, will shatter the stereotypes into which we have either been imprisoned, or into which we have incarcerated ourselves. Equally compelling is the case for the legacy we can leave our daughters and granddaughters. While we may not directly discourage them from domesticity, we can certainly point them to the "better part" as our Conquering Hero did when visiting the home of sisters, Mary and Martha. Jesus was grateful, no doubt, for the lunch that Martha prepared for Him, but His accolade went to Mary, who couldn't get to the kitchen for eating up His words.[12]

Jesus promised that when we choose intimacy over intimidation, the majestic over the mundane, His approval over that of all others, His great inheritance would never be taken away from us. The Lord Jesus Christ blazed the trail for emancipation throughout His earthly tenure; He paid for it conclusively by His death and, through His resurrection, imbued us with His very own life. Our liberty came at a great price. The greatest gesture of gratitude we can show Him is to run rejoicing, forever free.

Nourishing Nuggets from *The Message:*

"In Christ's family there can be no division into Jew and non-Jew, slave and free, male and female. Among us you are all equal. That is, we are all in a common relationship with Jesus Christ" (Galatians 3).

"So if the Son sets you free, you are free through and through" (John 8).

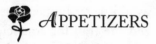 ***A*PPETIZERS**

❶ *A thankful heart cultivates contentment.*

❷ *No matter what materials life has allotted you—gold, silver, wood, or straw—your reward at the end of the day will be based on how you have built on the foundation of faith in Christ Jesus.*

12

Contentment
In Christ

AN AMUSING ANECDOTE is told of a very old lady who was asked if she was content, to which she replied, "I will be, once I see my daughter safely settled in a nursing home." A hovering mama to the bitter end!

Blessedly, we can come to contentment sooner than this dear lady did; serenity is not the exclusive domain of the old. If we learn to relinquish our god-like grasp, we can enjoy the bliss of contentment throughout our mothering years from the deluge of diapers to high school graduation day; even to end-of-life concerns should we outlive our children.

Cultivating Contentment

"There is great gain in godliness combined with content-ment" (1 Timothy 6:6). Our family used this verse of scripture in my dad's obituary when he died. In his golden years he grew mellow, tranquil, trusting, and great godliness shone through. The life of Christ in us guarantees our godliness at any age. With that given, cultivating contentment is our responsibility.

Our discontent derives from unthankfulness. We murmur and grumble when we lose our sense of gratitude, always want-ing something bigger or better—a larger house, a child of another gender, or a smarter and prettier one. If we travel often to the wishing well, we lose sight of the deep supply that the present moment provides. As well as disturbing our own peace, the lives of our children are deeply affected by an attitude of ingratitude. Children cannot edit information and impressions. Our restlessness may well register as our disappointment in them and make them feel they are an intrusion and an obstacle to our finding contentment.

When we feel overwhelmed, our disquietude may simply be the result of succumbing to the temptation to wish that our little ones were more mature, less dependent, or grown and gone. Whether we have ever considered it as such, each of these complaints constitutes discontent. We are in danger of forgetting that everyday events make up the big picture; God has given us a ream of time cut off in measures of one day, and grumbling gives us a heads-up that we have lost sight of the perfect plan and provision of the parenthood of God.

Even if we are quite satisfied with our lot, and life lopes along in unperturbed equilibrium, what happens when life crashes? We object strenuously to the possibility that we can know serenity when things are not so smooth, but that is when our self-sufficiency usually shatters and we are compelled to turn to the Life within for our serenity. As Henri Nouwen has said:

> Our brokenness opened us to a deeper way of sharing
> our lives and offering each other hope. Just as bread
> needs to be broken in order to be given, so, too, do our
> lives.[1]

A mother's life is full of broken things—from a tot's broken toys to a teen's broken heart over a first love, to the tragedy of a car wreck that leaves a child crippled or dead. Later, perhaps the divorce of an adult child dashes our dreams for the ideal, happy family. When this happens, we are tempted to conclude that, if only we had done everything "right," our family would have turned out differently. Instead of resorting to recrimination and resentment, if we consider the faithfulness of God in turning all things to good, this will help us see brokenness as a blessing that cannot disturb our peace.

God's Patient Grace

Have you ever thought about God's historical household? The record shows anything but a trouble-free, fully functioning, felicitous family. Adam and Eve didn't exactly model marital harmony. And their boys, Cain and Abel, endowed us with sibling rivalry, a legacy that we could have done without. Abraham, the great father of faith was not above twisting the truth at the expense of his wife. And David, the king of Israel, was a murderer and adulterer who spawned a drastically dysfunctional family. Recall also Rebecca, the model for manipulative motherhood. Even the family into which Jesus was born would raise a few eyebrows in religious circles today. His mother was an unwed, pregnant teenager who eventually married the man who became Jesus' step-dad. (Point to ponder here: Mary's great love and devotion to that child could not keep Him from an unjust, untimely and hideous death; she could not keep Him from the pre-ordained plan of His Father.)

How gracious of God to touch all the bases of our experiences, identify with our humanity and make sure it was recorded for posterity, so silencing those who insist that we must have a perfect family to show forth a good testimony for God.

His testimony to us is more important than our testimony of Him. He maintained His undisturbed contentment throughout the millennia, because He was confident that Christ would complete everyone and everything, in the appropriate time.

What a relief.

We may spend our entire lives trying to produce the flawless family, our peace and tranquility remaining a mirage that never materializes in the desert of discontent. We think of certain choices that our children could make that would reflect our spiritual success, such as full-time ministry. In times past, for example, the epitome of spirituality in an Irish family was to have a son or daughter choose the church, become a priest or a nun. The other day in the gym, I overheard a couple of moms, with swelling pride, swapping stories of how their daughters and sons were "working for the Lord." Those who have prodigals might fall silent during such a conversation, feeling they have failed.

Love, the Lasting Measure

Only love never fails. God's love for us and through us never fails. Our assignment on the earth is to learn that love. His is a love which brings undisturbed peace, no matter what. "It is trusting enough in Jesus to make mistakes and believing enough that His life will still pulse within us," writes Brennan Manning.[2] And in that immense expanse of life called Christ, we can rest. There is a divine injunction to entering rest, for only then do we surrender control and engage contentment, no matter what the circumstances. This is what the apostle Paul meant when he said he had learned the secret of contentment; whether in want or plenty, Christ Jesus was his supply.[3]

We may have wanted things to be very different in our mothering lives. I've concluded that trying to define life within the parameters of human time is doomed to disappointment. There is so much more purpose than we can envision with our limited perspective. Pain, regret, and disillusionment may dot the landscapes of our lives like exploded mines we wish we had avoided. What we cannot avoid is God's ecstatic love for us and His provision for our unmitigated joy and contentment in Christ. In His eyes we are not defined by our productivity or success as society or religion sees it, but by our acceptance in the Beloved. The bliss of cradling a newborn or the hugging of a graduate marks neither the beginning nor end of our lives. No amount of mothering or managing a career can compare to what our heavenly Father has accomplished in us, and what He will complete right up to the end.

As we keep that in focus, we must bear in mind that we will have to give an accounting for our lives. We will stand alone, not as wife, worker, or mother. There will be no husband to stand by our side either to vouch for us or to criticize us; no employer with a glowing reference in hand and no children to tout for our fortitude, fairness, or failures. We will not be measured against expectations, tradition, or duty, but by what we have done with Christ Jesus. Some of us have had easier roads to travel, our tools and talents of gold and silver caliber; others a hard and grueling journey with meager supplies of hay and straw. No matter what materials we have had at our disposal, their value will be assessed only to the degree that we have used them in reliance on the completed work of Christ.

Driving through the stunning beauty of Bavaria, Germany several years ago, I was in a reflective mood, ready to listen to my God rather than just talk to Him. Taking a break from the heady, full, and fulfilling life of ministry I was in at the time, I wondered just how my work would stand the test at the end of the day. I simply breathed, "Lord, what is it that will really count, in your estimation?"

Softly and surely, He reminded me of the well-known passage of scripture in 1 Corinthians chapter 13. After all our great efforts, achievements, and accolades are over, the writer, the Apostle Paul, sums up by saying, "And the greatest of these is love." Love is the lasting measure of all our work.

With few exceptions, that is the lifetime quest of a mother's heart. We want the highest and best for our children. As we have learned throughout this book, the longing for perfect love will lead us straight into the arms of our heavenly Parent. There, all the mothering mantras, state-of-the-art parenting techniques, and latest child raising rubrics come to completion in God's limitless love. As the thirteenth-century theologian Anthony of Padua wrote, "Of what value is learning that does not turn to love?"

So, on our heavenly graduation day, we can look forward to standing confidently before our gracious God. We will receive our recompense, not for simply being a biological mother, or by looking to our children's destiny to count to our credit, but for being a woman who identified with Christ. We will be rewarded for being a woman whose contentment was consistently in Him alone, and who relied on a love greater than her own for the precious charges that are her children. We trusted in the God who is everywhere—for a god we could never be.

Nourishing Nuggets from *The Message:*

"I've learned by now to be quite content whatever my circumstances. Whatever I have, wherever I am, I can make it through anything in the One who makes me who I am" (Philippians 4).

"Trust steadily in God, hope unswervingly, love extravagantly. And the best of the three is love" (1 Corinthians 13).

Appendix 1:

Voices that Vote

What follows is a compilation of several mothers' reflections, ruminations, and reliances on God. In their own words these mothers reveal a wide variety of emotions, experiences, and challenges with children. They are selected in the hope that you can identify with some of their situations; that you will feel validated, encouraged, and confident in the faithfulness of your glorious God.

The writers remain anonymous to you, the reader, but not to their Lord. They are the brave, the courageous, the compassionate hearts whom He knows well. He has held them to His bosom, reached out to them in the dark watches of the night, and bottled their tears. I salute them, thank them, and love them.

MOTHER #1:

"Loved Like My Own"

As an adoptive mother, I am often asked, "Why adopt?" Before I can answer their question, people have their own assumptions ready: "Is it because you couldn't have your own? Were you trying to rescue a child?" and many others. The simplest answer for me to give is, "Because I could; I wanted to; so I did."

"So what does it feel like?" ... "Is it working out?"

113

These questions often follow. I love my daughter; so yes, it is working out, whatever that means. She is more than I hoped for. She is affectionate and so willing to embrace our family values. However, adoption is not without its difficulties. She joined our family at the age of nine with a history littered with hurt, betrayal, pain, and numerous disruptions. However, she had also been the beneficiary of friendship and love from adults who cared for her.

Though my emotions have gone up and down, I can say that I have loved her before I met her, the way a natural mother loves the child in her womb. This child was in my mind; I knew her details and history and grew to love her. When she arrived, I was conscious that my love was measured, at first, because I was afraid. What if she did not like me? However, as the days turned into weeks and the weeks into months, so my love deepened.

She sometimes cries about her past and my heart breaks with her. I try to encourage her with the words that Joseph, in the Old Testament, said to his brothers who had rejected him: "What you meant for evil, God has turned for good." My daughter has a future. We will make every opportunity available to her so that she can reach her full potential. That is what spurs this mother on.

MOTHER #2:
"The Pain of Alone"

"I sat alone at lunch again, Mom," said my child coming off the bus with head down and noticeably missing his huge smile and twinkling brown eyes.

These words, more than any others, grip at this mother's heart. My son, Josh, began middle school and now finds that he is surrounded more by strangers than by friends. Although he is an extremely gregarious boy, he is no longer around the kids with whom he shared six years of elementary school. He was diagnosed with Traumatic Brain Injury and has trouble with social cues, memory, sequencing, fine motor skills and impulsiveness. School is the last thing on Josh's list of priorities—he would much rather be hiking in the mountains, riding his bike, or chasing deer around the property.

I had unusual premonitions about this child while he was still in diapers. By the age of three, his vocabulary was extremely limited and he would act out his frustrations in horrific head banging sessions. I remember just holding him with tears streaming, feeling the depths of compassion, frustration, anger, and pity. Emotions were mixed and rampant in those early days. I asked questions like, "Why would God give me this challenge; I'm not up to it" and "Why did my son have these cards dealt him?"

I have received no answers. All I know is that God has asked me to love this creation of His and to trust that He is in control and has a plan for all lives that come into contact with Josh, mine included. Those kids who are choosing not to sit with him at lunch don't know the blessing they are missing.

MOTHER #3:
"I'm a Mama Once More"

At the time I was thrust back into motherhood, after preparing myself for the empty nest, I rebelled for a while. I was physically tired from raising my own kids and I was looking forward to doing my own thing. Not that I did not love this beautiful grandbaby that I grew to love the moment she was born. (I was in the delivery room with her and was the first one to hold her). However, those were not my plans for retirement. After talking through my anger and resentment to my heavenly father,

He told me that to take care of this grandchild would be like worship unto Him.

Settled with that in my mind, it truly became a joy to raise another child. She is her grandma and grandpa's sunshine; sometimes also a challenge, but—through Christ who strengthens me—all things are possible. Originally, we only planned to have her in our care until her mother finished college, but His hand again altered these plans. So, five and a half years later we are still raising our granddaughter. Although I have lost friends of my own age, she has kept this senior citizen young, going to school activities and being a part of all the wonderful things young children do. My life would truly have a huge void if it were not for her.

Up to the present, we have had no major conflict with her mother and have asked her permission to adopt our granddaughter. I feel blessed to teach her the things of the Lord and she has asked Christ to come into her life. This little girl's presence in our family has been a great blessing and a tool in the Father's hands to reach my husband with the love of God. I can only say that the Father is truly in control; we are not. We might make our plans, but the outcome is in His hands. The sooner we acknowledge Him in all areas of our lives, the more joyful the journey.

MOTHER #4:
"Mother of Many"

I am the mother of eight children and fifteen grandchildren. In 57 years of marriage I have learned many things. Among these, patience, the willingness to listen, and the ability to be organized are invaluable. I found that when I ordered my home well, life with eight children ran smoothly and happily and home was a place of peace and comfort.

When my children disappointed me, I found that my feelings of failure subsided when I realized that I had done the best I could. They have free will and are responsible for their own actions. With many children come many opportunities for disappointments, sicknesses and trials.

On one particular occasion, when my mother was near death following surgery, my husband's hand was lost in an accident. At the time, it looked like his sight would be damaged too. I had to take my two children under three and travel four hours in a bus to see him in the hospital. As I was being told of the extent of their daddy's injuries, I felt the presence of my sweet Jesus physically standing beside me, and I felt his hand on my shoulder.

All my children are blessings from the Lord, especially my two, brain-injured sons. I offer all my sufferings to Him whose love I trust, whose help is always available, and on whom I can utterly rely in every trial.

MOTHER #5:
"Hope in Homosexuality"

I am the mother of a daughter who thinks she is a lesbian; or rather, she sees that as her identity. I see her identity as a person in Christ because she accepted Christ as her Savior when a teenager. I have to see through this situation as I would any other, and see the potential of Christ in her, otherwise I would have no hope. In the world, I see that we attach more importance to some sins than others; and the sexual sins seem to top the list. My daughter's false identity is no worse than if she were living with a male partner outside of marriage.

The hardest thing for me now is not her situation, but what seems to be her rejection of me. I realize that her false identity is born out of her experiences and is part of her training. It is also the Father's way of training me. I have to work at remembering that I am not at fault and to put the guilt where it belongs. This present, false identity is her choice—she was not born that way.

I am now focusing more on my own life, rather than centering my life in hers. Only when I forget that my true identity is in Christ, do I start looking for my life's affirmation in my daughter. My old self wants to rise up in this situation and be hurt. Feelings are deceptive and I have learned to step back and look long and hard until the feelings pass. God certainly is there, and I will have to wait on His time and stay out of His way.

I'm not quite to the rejoicing part, but that will come.

MOTHER #6:
"Both Ends of the Spectrum"

My first child was perfect, coming into the world with eyes eager to absorb every new thing he saw. For the first many weeks, my husband and I just watched him in awe. That such a miracle had come from us was almost more than we could believe. Yet, I remember in those early days, when the sun was setting and the feelings of melancholy brushed against my heart, how sad I felt for the days to come when he might not be picked for a team on the playground. Silly it seemed, as I watched this infant gift.

My second child was perfect; what mother doesn't think so? Not long after his very vocal entrance to the world, he became very quiet. He was quiet for his first years, watching but not engaging, slow to lift his head, crawl, and walk. While his big brother was using words and humor as a young master craftsman, he just watched. It was hard to tell what was going into his mind and what wasn't. One child born gifted; one child born with processing deficiencies.

One child with special needs? No, both had special needs.

For, while the articulate child was off the chart with intelligence, he was different. Unlike the "normal" kids who are athletic and given to the group mentality, he thrived on one-to-one attention and enjoyed batting ideas rather than balls. And the "normal" kids were quick to point out his differences. His younger brother's differences were evident, too, as he struggled to focus and then to retain. He began to pull into himself and feared interactions with others, because it was hard for him to understand it all. The nuances of interaction eluded him, so he remained quiet and distant.

Neither of our boys was quickly chosen for teams. There is a longing in a mother's heart for her children to "fit in." When I saw my older one not able to even catch a ball well, I would get angry and make him throw the ball with me. I tried endlessly to get my youngest to focus, when it was chemically impossible. By the grace of God, the same parents, the same womb produced two radically different human beings. And while so often I have longed to be able to fit them into the mainstream of humanity, they constantly remind me that our Creator has crafted each one of us differently, not to fit into a mainstream, but to fit with Him.

And while I have not mastered relinquishing that desire for them to fit, which truthfully is not only for their own sakes but also for mine, when I look at them and who they are, I sometimes delight in them as their heavenly Father does. Then, I have a sense that my own "not fitting" is also a part of His plan to have me as His own.

MOTHER #7:
"Returned to Sender"

The couple, who had sat waiting patiently for me to wrap up work in my restaurant kitchen, finally faced me across the table. They asked me if February 28, 1969 meant anything to me. At that, the closed door of my heart came crashing open.

The little girl I had given up for adoption, was now twenty years old and looking for her birth mother. The baby girl, that I had only looked at once as she lay in the hospital nursery, wanted to know her blood family. Her adoptive father had died and her adoptive mother was quite dysfunctional. Up until that time, no one but my husband knew of this child's existence. But when they found out, my huge family threw a party, and embraced her as their own. She would later tell me that the one thing she had always felt at her adoptive family's gatherings was that no one looked like her.

Although I was thrilled to be reconnected with my daughter, I was crushed under the most terrible weight of condemnation. I was crying at work, in the shower; my soul was just bereft. I was mourning for the baby girl that I never held and I was putting myself through a really bad time. The category into which I put myself was the mother with the great big scarlet "A" on her chest, especially as I walked down the aisle at her wedding a few months later. However, instead of judgment, I felt love from the 300 pairs of eyes trained on my entrance. Our friends were thrilled that Julie had found her mother and that I had found my little girl.

Just when the guilt and shame were becoming too much, God whispered sweetly to me in the tear-soaked shower, "I forgave you a long time ago, but you have never forgiven yourself." Words cannot express how glad I am for God's love that brought us together again. With His help, I am going to remember that He forgave me at the Cross, and no one, not even I, can condemn me anymore!

APPENDIX 2:

Reading Resources

HERE IS A LIST of titles that will enhance your understanding of some of the positions espoused in this book. They are permanent fixtures in my personal library and I am drawn time after time to many of them for the solace and assurance I need when I forget that God is truly God. When I am frustrated, feeble, and floundering in a sea of conflicting waves of thought, I come back to the solid ground of the shore, where my Savior awaits. He assures me of His sufficiency, reminding me, one more time, that I can do nothing without Him, but all things I am called to do in Him. May these prove a sweet addition to your source of books that bless.

Adams, Kenneth M. PhD. *Silently Seduced: When Parents Make Their Children Partners, Understanding Covert Incest.* Deerfield Beach, Florida: Health Communications, Inc., 1991.

Bristow, John Temple. *What Paul Really Said About Women: An Apostle's Liberating Views on Equality in Marriage, Leadership, and Love.* San Francisco: Harper Collins, 1988.

George, Bob. *Complete in Christ: Discovering God's View of You.* Eugene: Harvest House, 1994.

Julian of Norwich. *Enfolded in Love: Daily Readings with Julian of Norwich,* 12th Reprint. London: Darton, Longman and Todd Ltd., 1990.

Kroeger, Richard and Catherine Clark. *I Suffer not A Woman: Rethinking 1 Timothy 2:11-15 In Light of Ancient Evidence.* Grand Rapids: Baker Books, 1992.

Litzman, Warren. *The Making of a Son*. Dallas: Christ-Life Publishing House, 1993.

Longman, Ernest and Marion. *Shared Love: A Sunrise of Hope for Personal Relationships*. Farwell: Jacobs Ladder Printing, 1998.

Manning, Brennan. *Abba's Child: The Cry of the Heart for Intimate Belonging*. Colorado Springs: Navpress, 1994.

Nee, Watchman. *Christ The Sum of All Spiritual Things* (translated from the Chinese). New York: Christian Fellowship Publishers, Inc., 1973.

Nouwen, Henri J.M. *The Return of The Prodigal Son: A Story of Homecoming*. New York: Image Books, Doubleday, 1992.
———. *Life of the Beloved: Spiritual Living in a Secular World*. New York: Crossroad, 1996.

Smith, Paul R. *Is It Okay To Call God "Mother"?: Considering the Feminine Face of God*. Peabody: Hendrickson Publishers, 1995.

Volkman, Bill. *Basking In His Presence: A Call to the Prayer of Silence*. Grand Rapids: Dickinson Press, 1996.

Notes

FOREWORD
1. Gal. 2:19b, 20.

ONE—MOTHERHOOD: HISTORY AND HOPE
1. Gen. 3:4-5.
2. E. B. White, *Charlotte's Web* (New York: Scholastic Book Services, 1952), 144.
3. 1 Pet. 4:8.
4. Bret Lott, *Jewel* (New York: Washington Square Press, 1991).
5. Sarah Blaffer Hrdy, 1999, *Mother Nature: A History of Mothers, Infants and Natural Selection*, Quoting from *Herbert Spencer, An Autobiography, Vol. I* (New York: D Appleton, 1904), 13-14.
6. Ibid., Quoting from George Eliot, *Adam Bede* (London: Penguin Books, 1989), 17.
7. Elizabeth Fox Genovese et al, *Women and the Future of the Family* (Grand Rapids: Baker Books, 2000), 70.
8. Gal. 3:28.
9. Alvin J Schmidt, *Veiled and Silenced: How Culture Shaped Sexist Theology* (Macon: Mercer University Press, 1980), 88-89.
10. Richard Clark Kroeger and Catherine Clark Kroeger, *I Suffer Not a Woman: Rethinking 1 Timothy 2:11-15 In Light of Ancient Evidence* (Grand Rapids: Baker Books, 1992), 171-177.

TWO—ONLY ONE IS PERFECT AND HE IS IN YOU
1. Kathy Collard Miller, *When Counting to 10 Isn't Enough: Defusing Anger* (Wheaton: Harold Shaw, 1996), 35-36.
2. Brenda Hunter, PhD, *The Power of Mother Love: Transforming Both Mother and Child* (Colorado Springs: Waterbrook Press, 1997), 55.
3. Psalm 27:10
4. Anonymous via Email.
5. *Billy Elliot,* screenplay by Lee Hall, directed by Stephen Daldry (Copyright 2000, Universal Studios).

THREE—HELICOPTER MOM, YOU'RE CREATING A DRAFT
1. Ariel Gore and Bee Lavender, *Breeder: Real-Life Stories from the New Generation of Mothers* (Seattle: Seal Press, 2001), 126.
2. Kenneth M. Adams, PhD., *Silently Seduced: When Parents Make Their Children Partners, Understanding Covert Incest* (Deerfield Beach: Health Communications, Inc., 1991), back cover.
3. Carolyn Warner, *Treasury of Women's Quotations* (1992, quoting Dorothy Canfield Fisher—1879-1958), p. 118.

FOUR—KEEPING UP APPEARANCES
1. *Keeping up Appearances*, written by Roy Clarke, produced by Harold Snoad. BBC Television, copyright TV Resources, 1997-2001.
2. Alice Miller, *The Drama of The Gifted Child: The Search for the True Self*, (New York: Basic Books, 1997), 30.
3. Exod. 33:4-6.
4. Erma Bombeck. *God's Choice of Mothers.* UNIVERSAL PRESS SYNDICATE, May 1980.
5. Henri J. M. Nouwen, *The Return of the Prodigal Son: A Story of Homecoming* (New York: Image Book, 1992), 98-99.
6. Ibid., 42-43.
7. Richard Wurmbrand, *From the Lips of Children*, (London: Hodder and Stoughton, 1986), 162.
8. 1 Tim. 1:19,20; 2 Tim. 4:14; Acts 15:37-40.

FIVE—CLAIMING YOUR OWN IDENTITY
1. Danielle Crittenden, *What Our Mothers Didn't Tell Us: Why Happiness Eludes The Modern Woman* (New York: Simon and Schuster, 1999), 60-61.
2. Sara Ban Breathnach, *Something More: Excavating Your Authentic Self* (New York: Warner Books, 1998), 53.
3. Gal. 2:20.
4. Helen B. Andelin, *Fascinating Womanhood* (New York: Bantam Doubleday, 1975).
5. John 16:13-14.
6. Joan Anderson, *A Year by The Sea, Thoughts of an Unfinished Woman* (New York; Broadway Books, 1999), back cover.

SIX—WHEN BOTH YOU AND THEY MAKE MISTAKES
1. Rom. 7:8-11.
2. Genesis 50:20.
3. Julian of Norwich, *Enfolded in Love* (London: Darton, Longman and Todd, 1980), 17.
4. 2 Cor. 12:9-10.
5. 1 Kings 10:7.

SEVEN—THE SOUND OF SILENCE
1. Danielle Crittenden, *What our Mothers Didn't Tell Us: Why Happiness Eludes The Modern Woman* (New York: Simon and Schuster, 1999), 141.
2. Carolyn Warner, *Treasury of Women's Quotations* (Englewood Cliffs: Prentice Hall, 1992), quoting Jacqueline Kennedy Onassis, 322.

EIGHT—NO MEDDLING ZONE
1. Job 32:6-9.
2. Madeleine L'Engle, *A Circle of Quiet: The Crossroads Journal, Book One* (San Francisco: Harper Collins, 1972), 46.
3. Nancy Parker Brummett, *It Takes a Home: And Other Lessons from the Heart* (Colorado Springs: Cook Communications, 2000), 203.
4. Carolyn G. Heilbrun, *The Last Gift of Time: Life Beyond Sixty*, (New York: Ballantyne Books, 1997), 187.
5. 1 Pet. 4:8.

NINE—DEALING WITH DADS
1. Ernest and Marion Longman, *Shared Love: A Sunrise of Hope for Relationships* (Farwell: Jacobs Ladder Printing, 1998) 101.
2. Paul R. Smith, *Is It Okay to Call God "Mother": Considering the Feminine Face of God* (Peabody: Hendrickson Publishers) 201.
3. W. Ward Gasque, *"The Role of Women In The Church, In Society and In The Home," The Priscilla Papers*, Vol. 12, Number 1, (Winter 1998), 17.
4. Ruth Haley Barton, *Equal To The Task: Men & Women In Partnership* (Downers Grove, Ill. InterVarsity Press: 1998), 173.

TEN—SHEDDING THE SKIN OF GUILT
1. *Webster's Ninth New College Dictionary* (Springfield: Merriam Webster Inc., 1991) 542.
2. 1 John 1:9.
3. William Glasser, M. D., *Stations of The Mind: New Directions for Reality Therapy* (New York: Harper and Row, 1981), 161-62.
4. Matt. 25:40.
5. Compton, K. C, 2001, *Have a Heart: Natural Awakenings* (February 2001), 18, quoting Stephen Sinatra, M. D.
6. John chapter 21.

ELEVEN—SHATTERING THE STEREOTYPES
1. Mark 5:25-34.
2. Lev. 15:19-30.
3. Luke 7:36-50.
4. John 4:4-42.
5. Psalm 18:2; Rev. 5:5.
6. Isa. 42:14.
7. Isa. 66:12,13.
8. 1 Pet. 1:23.
9. John 8:58.
10. Job 42:15.
11. Job 42:15.
12. Luke 10:38-42.

TWELVE—CONTENTMENT IN CHRIST
1. Henri J. M. Nouwen, *Life of the Beloved: Spiritual Living in a Secular World* (New York: Crossroad, 1996), 88.
2. Brennan Manning, *Abba's Child: The Cry of the Heart for Intimate Belonging* (Colorado Springs, NavPress, 1994), 138.
3. Phil. 4:11.

Acknowledgments

I owe the deepest gratitude to...

🌹 The many mothers who kindly and candidly shared their hearts, hopes, and insights.

🌹 My fellow writers who read, critiqued, and contributed to many of the chapters;

🌹 Those who painstakingly edited the entire work with me.

🌹 The technical expert, the patient and constant collaborator, my husband, Jim.

~ *Alice Scott-Ferguson*

About the Author

Alice Scott-Ferguson is a Scottish-born freelance writer and motivational speaker. She was educated as a registered nurse in Scotland, holds a B.S. in Health Sciences, and has worked mainly in the psychiatric field.

She has contributed to both the secular and religious press, has authored several Bible studies and written prize-winning poetry. Her first book *Little Women, Big God* was published in 1999 and is the story of the women's ministry she founded and directed in the U.K.

An engaging and enthusiastic speaker, Alice has traveled internationally, presenting at various venues—women's seminars, writers workshops, and conferences for both women and men. She is passionately committed to bring God's liberating love and freedom to her audience. She continues to lead several Bible study classes each week locally and her passion is ever to teach and live out the fierce, limitless love of God.

Mothers Can't Be Everywhere, But God Is was first released by Cladach Publishing in 2002. Then Alice co-authored, with Nancy Parker Brummett, *Reconcilable Differences: Two Friends Debate God's Role for Women* (2006, David C. Cook)

A collection of Alice's poetry, *Pausing in the Passing Places*, was released in 2018 by Cladach Publishing.

Alice was widowed a few years ago and has recently remarried. Her family has now extended to include four step children and nine step grandchildren in addition to her own three natural children and six grandchildren who are scattered across the country.

Alice and her husband live in Phoenix, Arizona.

9 780967 038674